T

P9-APN-377

# LAWRENCE OF ARABIA
## and his world

RICHARD PERCEVAL GRAVES

# LAWRENCE OF ARABIA

## and his world

CHARLES SCRIBNER'S SONS

NEW YORK

The author's grateful thanks are due to
Professor A. W. Lawrence and the Trustees of
the T. E. Lawrence Letters Trust for special
permission for the use of hitherto unpublished
material and to the Trustees of the Seven
Pillars of Wisdom Trust for the use of
quotations from that work.

For the use of other unpublished material, the
author's thanks are due to Miss Farida el Akle,
Mr Tom Beaumont, Mrs R. C. Chilver,
Mr John Graves, Mr George Hilton and
Mrs Hilda Sims.

1 3 5 7 9 11 13 15 17 19 I/C 20 18 16 14 12 10 8 6 4 2

Printed in Great Britain
Library of Congress Catalog Card Number 76–7183
ISBN 0–684–14726–2

*For my dear wife,* ANNE

*Imagination should be put into*
*the most precious caskets, and*
*that is why one can only live in*
*the future or the past, in Utopia*
*or the Wood beyond the World.*

T. E. Lawrence,
in a letter to his mother.

*. . . ye of the world beyond the*
*Mountains are stronger and more*
*godlike than we, as all tales*
*tell; and ye wear away your*
*lives desiring that which ye*
*may scarce get. . . . Therefore*
*ye know sickness and sorrow,*
*and oft ye die before your time.*

from *The Well at the World's End*
by William Morris

IN OCTOBER 1917 GREAT BRITAIN had been at war with Germany for three years; and, as part of that war, she had encouraged and supported an Arab Revolt against Turkey, one of Germany's allies. A young Englishman, Thomas Edward Lawrence, was blowing up Turkish trains on the Damascus–Medina railway line; and rumours of his success were spreading rapidly through the scattered Arabian tribes. 'Send us a lurens', wrote the Beni Atiyeh to Feisal, son of the Sherif of Mecca who had raised the Revolt, 'and we will blow up trains with it.' 'Lurens' became a legend not only in Arabia, but in the west; and the story of his life has fascinated readers and writers ever since.

He was born in the peaceful Welsh village of Tremadoc on 16 August 1888, the illegitimate second son of a wealthy Anglo-Irish landowner, Thomas Chapman, and a Scottish governess, Sarah Maden, with whom he had run away from his wife and daughters. To escape the censure of the middle-class society of Victorian Britain, they changed their names to Lawrence by deed poll, and made constant moves. By the time that he was eight, Ned, as his family called him, had lived in Wales, Scotland, the Isle of Man, Jersey, France and southern England. It was only then that Mr and Mrs Lawrence, now with four sons, felt safe enough to settle down at 2 Polstead Road, Oxford.

'Woodlands', Tremadoc, the birthplace of T. E. Lawrence.

Ned's early childhood was neither remarkable nor strange. He was strong, active, intelligent and self-possessed. He went to the Oxford High School where, on his first day in the Lower IV, a boy sitting next to him began to gloat over the fact that he was one day older than Lawrence. Ned retorted that this was unfortunate, since it prevented the boy from being born on Napoleon's birthday, as he was. He hated bullying of any sort, and it was when he had gone to the rescue of a boy who was being bullied in the school playground that he had the fall which broke a bone in his leg and according to his mother halted his growth.

He did not care much for his formal education, but his father had encouraged him to take up brass-rubbing at the age of ten, and he became increasingly fascinated by the medieval world. With school friends he went to meetings of the Oxford Archaeological Society, toured the neighbouring villages making brass-rubbings, traced the passage of a medieval sewer, and searched in the libraries for the histories of priests and knights and ladies.

Bob, Will and Ned Lawrence as boys, with Frank Lawrence as a baby. Sarah Lawrence recalled that her sons were 'a most happy band of brothers'; and by the time he was six, Ned was their leader. Will was probably his favourite brother, but when Arnold was born – the youngest by twelve years – he showed him the special affection an older child may sometimes feel for a much younger brother or sister.

The City of Oxford High School Sixth Form, 1906–7. The photograph includes Will Lawrence, middle of back row; and T.E., who actually took the picture, stands at the right with a bicycle pump activating the shutter release hidden under his jacket.

Oxford: the High.

9

He was sensitive enough to need peace and privacy, and when at the age of seventeen he felt that he could not get enough of either, he decided that further academic progress was impossible, and ran away to enlist as an ordinary soldier in the training battalion of the Royal Artillery. His father, whose private income was large enough for the Lawrence family to live comfortably upon it, bought him out after six months at a cost of £30, and built him a two-roomed bungalow at the bottom of their garden. Ned, or T.E. as he now liked to be called, sound-proofed the walls, and covered them with his brass-rubbings, Sir John d'Abernon, and Roger de Trumpington, a crusader, having pride of place.

During his last two years at school, T.E. did some valuable archaeological work at Oxford, paying workmen on a building site for finds of medieval pottery, glass and coins, and presenting them to the Ashmolean Museum. During the holidays he also made cycling tours around the medieval castles of Wales and France, sometimes covering enormous distances. When he had visited some family friends at Dinard, he reported: 'M. Corbeil was with them, and collapsed when he heard where I had come from. I had given them a topic of conversation for a week. Deux cent cinquante kilomètres. Ah la la, qu'il est merveilleux. Deux cent cinquante kilomètres . . .'

*Opposite*
Two of the numerous brass-rubbings made by T.E. as a schoolboy. *Left*, the effigy of Lord Beaumont in Wivenhoe church, Essex; *right*, Lord Berkeley, in the parish church of Wootton-under-Edge, Gloucestershire.

The bungalow which T.E.'s father built for him in the garden of their Oxford home.

Lawrence went up to Jesus College, Oxford, in October 1907 with a History Exhibition. He spent one term in College, but was then allowed to live in his bungalow, which was now the centre of a world of old things. Another undergraduate, Vyvyan Richards, shared his delight in the best aspects of medieval life, and at one time they planned to build a medieval hall in Epping Forest, where they would produce hand-printed books of exceptional quality. Richards later admitted that he had been physically attracted to Lawrence; but the feelings were not reciprocated by T.E., who appreciated his enthusiasm and craftsmanship, but described him as a difficult personality.

Sir Ernest Barker, Lawrence's tutor in medieval history, found him 'like lightning, zig-zag and instantaneous'. He had an independent and original outlook which owed much to his habit of reading widely round any subject which he was studying. His own preference was for medieval sagas and romances, and sometimes he would read until dawn, 'wandering for hours in the forest with Percivale or Sagramors le desirous'. There was a tougher and more gregarious side to Lawrence: he tested himself to the limits, making himself independent of regular food and sleep, swimming on frozen winter nights, and bicycling non-stop until he collapsed with exhaustion; he also joined in the traditional college battles

The town of Chipping Campden, at about the time when T.E. and Vyvyan Richards stayed there on a 'pilgrimage in honour of William Morris'. They visited the Morris house at Broad Campden, and saw the great Morris–Burne Jones Chaucer.

between rival groups of undergraduates. He was keenly interested in photography, and he practised with a pistol until he was a good shot with either hand.

Sarah Lawrence's guilt about living with another woman's husband encouraged her to be a strict Christian; under her influence the Lawrence family were regular worshippers, and regarded the rector of St Aldate's church, Canon Christopher, as a personal friend. He did them a service by asking D. G. Hogarth, a Fellow of Magdalen College and Curator of the Ashmolean Museum, to keep a friendly eye on T.E. while he was up at the University. Hogarth turned T.E.'s interests in the direction of the Middle East, so that as a thesis for his degree he decided to write about the military architecture of the Crusades. He took lessons in simple Arabic, and talked to Charles Doughty, famous traveller and author of what was now Lawrence's favourite book, *Travels in Arabia Deserta*. In the summer of 1909 he went out to Syria, where he walked the land from Beirut to Haifa and from Acre to Aleppo, gathering material for his thesis and living like an Arab. It was a dangerous journey, and on one occasion he was beaten by Kurds and left for dead; but in many villages he found a warm welcome.

'When I go into a native house', he wrote, 'the owner salutes me, and I return it and then he says something to one of his

Canon Christopher, Rector of St Aldate's church, Oxford, where the Lawrence family were regular worshippers.

T.E.'s pen-and-ink sketch of Sahyun, one of the castles he visited on his journey through Syria in the summer of 1909.

SAHYUN. The South - East Corner.
tower of entrance is the furthest to the left. The great moat runs along before round tower on the right.

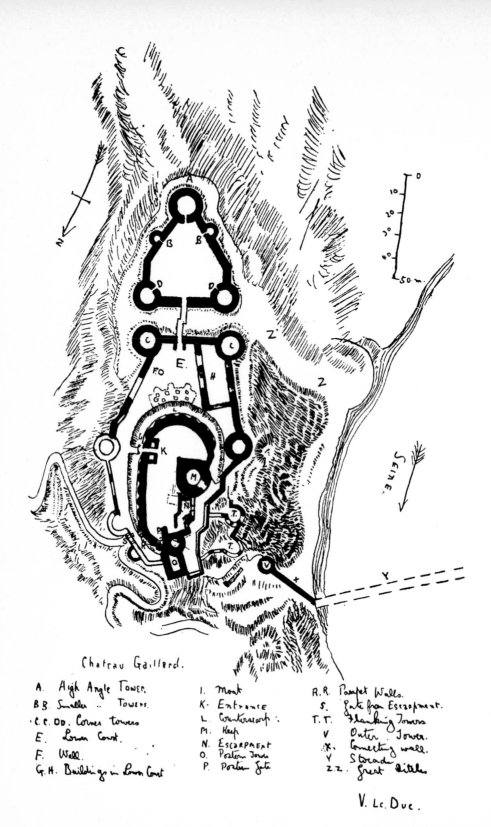

Chateau Gaillard.

A. High Angle Tower.
B B. Smaller .. Towers.
C C. DD. Corner towers
E. Lower Court.
F. Wall.
G. H. Buildings in Lower Court

I. Moat
K. Entrance
L. Counterscarp.
M. Keep
N. Escarpment
O. Postern Tower
P. Postern Gate

R.R. Parapet Walls.
S. Gate from Escarpment.
T.T. Flanking Towers
V. Outer Tower.
X. Connecting wall.
Y. Stocade
Z.Z. Great ditches

V. Le Duc.

Opposite
T.E.'s drawing of Château Gaillard, which he visited in the summer of 1907. He wrote then: 'The whole construction bears the unmistakeable stamp of genius. Richard I must have been a far greater man than we usually consider him: he must have been a great strategist and a great engineer, as well as a great man-at-arms.'

D. G. Hogarth, Keeper of the Ashmolean Museum and Fellow of Magdalen College, Oxford, who directed Lawrence's interests towards Middle Eastern archaeology.

women, and they bring out a thick quilt, which doubled is laid on the rush mat over the floor as a chair: on that I squat down, and then the host asks me four or five times how my health is, and each time I tell him that it is good. Then comes sometimes coffee, and after that a variety of questions, as to whether my [camera] tripod is a revolver, and what I am, and where I come from, and where I'm going, and why I'm on foot, and am I alone, and every other thing conceivable, and when I set up my tripod (sometimes, as a great treat) there are cries of astonishment, and "Mashallahs" "By the life of the Prophet", "Heavens", "Give God the glory" etc. etc. Such a curiosity has never been seen, and all the village is summoned to look at it.'

On his return to Oxford his thesis, later published as *Crusader Castles*, helped him to gain a First in Modern History.

Farida el Akle, an intelligent woman and a devout Christian, who was one of T.E.'s closest friends, and who still refers to him as 'Ned', the name by which his family knew him.

Lawrence came down from Oxford in June 1910; but Hogarth offered him fifteen shillings a day as an assistant in an expedition sponsored by the British Museum to uncover the ancient city of Carchemish on the bank of the Euphrates, and by the winter he was on his way back to Syria. On the journey he spent a few days at the heart of the Turkish Empire, Constantinople, the modern Istanbul. Here he admired the old Roman walls, and enjoyed the lively atmosphere, and the contrast between the bustle of the streets and the calm repose of the great mosques, with their wide cloisters in front of them paved with marble. When he arrived in Syria, he spent a couple of months studying Arabic at the American Mission school at Jebail, near Beirut. His teacher was Farida el Akle, a young Syrian woman whom he described as 'wonderful' in a letter to his parents. She returned his admiration, and Jebail became a second home for him during the next three years.

In February 1911 Lawrence travelled with Hogarth to Carchemish. He wrote that it was 'a most weird thing to be so far out of Europe; at Urfa and Deraah I have felt myself . . . away out of the Renaissance influence . . .'.

From this time until June 1914 he was back in England only at Christmas 1912 and for two weeks in July 1913. These were some of the happiest and most contented years of his life. It has been suggested that during this period he and Hogarth were in fact undercover agents, spying on the German bridge-building operations across the Euphrates. It is true that Lawrence told his parents he could see clearly at two miles' distance through a tele-photo lens; but he had been a keen amateur photographer since he was a schoolboy. There is no evidence that he was anything other than what he seemed: a young, clever, and enthusiastic archaeologist.

R. Campbell Thompson took over control of the dig in April 1911, but Lawrence did not follow Hogarth back to England. He stayed on to sort out pottery, take photographs and gradually, at the age of twenty-two, to assume control of the two hundred Arab workmen. They found him a congenial master: sometimes he set groups of them to compete against each other, and allowed them to fire off guns and pistols when they found anything of interest; sometimes he sat and talked to them as a friend for an hour or two. On one of T.E.'s visits to Jebail, Farida asked the Arab who accompanied him why Lawrence got on so well with his workers, and received the reply: 'He is one of us, there is nothing we do he cannot do, and he even excels us in doing it.' Lawrence was fascinated by Arab customs, and wrote with relish about a double wedding, which was preceded by the 'capture' of the brides-to-be:

Hill-top work at Carchemish.

'The grooms sit at home, in their houses, waiting for the women to come to them, & come they did in a great triumphal procession, everyone galloping or singing or shooting: the dowry carried before them on an ass in a great painted chest: and till late at night there was dancing to the music of hand-clapping, and shots being fired, and chanting to the pipes of such as were goat-herds or shepherds.'

The archaeologists ate fairly well except once when Haj, their cook, 'quite inadvertently emptied a curry tin into a pilaff! It was like eating peppered flames ...' There were more tedious annoyances, such as a plague of locusts: 'For three days the river was full of their bodies, and I could not take photographs for the air was silky in texture with the shimmering of all their wings'; and there were responsibilities, as the workers brought all their problems to Thompson and Lawrence. One man even asked them to pay the price, £12, for the town girl whom he wanted to buy; but they refused to help him, as 'he was quite poor, and could have got a girl from the villages round about for two pounds quite easily. And for that two pounds the girl would be very fat (a sign of beauty here) with lots of tattoo marks over her face, and able to make bread and knead dung-cakes for fuel.' Lawrence became very friendly with his foreman, Hamoudi, and took an elder-brotherly interest in Salim Ahmed. Ahmed was an eighteen-year-old donkey-boy nicknamed Dahoum, the dark one, because he was so fair; and he talked of using his wages to pay for schooling in Aleppo.

There were also visitors, notably the traveller Gertrude Bell. T.E. found her pleasant, though 'not beautiful (except with a veil on, perhaps)'. Having come straight from the German diggings at Kalaat Shirgat, she first told Thompson that his ideas of digging were prehistoric; but they showed her their finds, and then took her over such a range of subjects, including Byzantine, Crusader, Roman and Hittite architecture, Greek folk lore, Mesopotamian ethnology, Bronze Age metal technique, Anatole France, the Octobrists, and telephoto lenses, that 'she was quite glad to have her tea after an hour and a half'.

While the dig was suspended during the hot season of 1911, Lawrence went on a disastrous walk through northern Mesopotamia. It began interestingly enough, with a Sheikh who offered him 'two first-class wives in his gift', and with lessons in bread-making from women in the tiny village of Kassala. But later he suffered from an abscess at the roots of his wisdom teeth, and from dysentery; and his right instep collapsed. He made a rapid recovery, and at the beginning of 1912 he joined Flinders Petrie's dig in Egypt at Kafr Ammar, forty miles south of Cairo. 'A Petrie dig is a thing with a flavour of its own,' he wrote. 'Tinned kidneys

mingle with mummy-corpses and amulets in the soup: my bed is all gritty with prehistoric alabaster jars of unique types – and my feet at night keep the bread-box from the rats. For ten mornings in succession I have seen the sun rise as I breakfasted, and we came home at nightfall after lunching at the bottom of a 50-foot shaft, to draw pottery silhouettes, or string bead-necklaces. . . .' In his first week, they dug out about a hundred graves; and often, when the sun had set and it had grown suddenly cold, T.E. and his fellow workers wrapped themselves in the white linen cloth which had been buried in the Egyptian tombs, and walked home smelling of spices.

In the early spring Lawrence returned to Jerablus, the village near Carchemish, to oversee the building of the house where he and Leonard Woolley, the new director of the dig, were to live for the next two years. Woolley found that the Arabs suspected Lawrence of being sexually perverted because of his kindness to

Dahoum, Abd es Sala'am, Gregori and Hamoudi. Lawrence wrote in July 1911: 'I have had quite a success with our donkey-boy (Dahoum), who really is getting a glimmering of what a brain-storm is. He is beginning to use his reason as well as his intellect!'

T.E., Leonard Woolley, and workers, at Carchemish.

Dahoum. Apparently T.E. knew what the rumours were; but, as he knew that there was no truth in them, they appealed to his broad and sometimes rather mischievous sense of humour.

As the months went by, Lawrence was gradually losing interest in his undergraduate plans for the wooden hall in Epping Forest. He wrote several times to Vyvyan Richards, but the only enthusiastic note is struck when he mentions some detail of Arab life; and by December 1913 he was telling Richards that he liked his present way of life, and would probably continue in it. T.E. busied himself with teaching some of the Arabs multiplication tables, with defending the site at Carchemish from the German engineers who wished to use it as a quarry, and with working on a travel book, about Cairo, Smyrna, Constantinople, Beirut, Aleppo, Damascus and Medina. He had taught for some time in the Sunday school at St Aldate's, and Biblical quotations came easily to his mind. He remembered in his readings from the book of Proverbs: 'Wisdom hath builded her house, she hath hewn it out of seven pillars', and he decided to call his book about the seven cities *Seven Pillars of Wisdom*.

During working hours he was a noticeable figure on the site, wearing a grey blazer trimmed with pink, white shorts held up by a gaudy Arab belt with the swinging tassels of a bachelor, grey stockings, red slippers, and no hat. In the evening, he would add to this a gold-embroidered Arab waistcoat, and a cloak of gold and silver thread. In the hot seasons, he continued his wanderings in Arabia. He carried a revolver, and his hours of practice with it proved to be invaluable at least once. He was walking near Lalakia, when someone fired a shot at him. The bullet missed, and T.E. turned quickly, in time to see a man taking aim again, at a range of about fifty yards. Before the man could fire his second shot, Lawrence had drawn his own revolver and shot him in the right hand. He then walked up to the man, whom he now thought he recognized as a worker sacked by Hamoudi at Carchemish, tied up his wound, and sent him on his way with a kick.

When he went to England for a fortnight in the summer of 1913, he took Hamoudi and Dahoum with him. He refused to allow photographers to harass them, telling Hamoudi that he did not want to be 'the showman of two monkeys'. Returning to Carchemish, they continued with the excavations, one of the more exciting moments being when 'we found a great gateway, with long walls leading up to it, all lined with great carved slabs of black and white stone . . . a king and his children: men with drums and trumpets, and men dancing: a goddess at the head of a long procession of priests and priestesses carrying corn and vines and fruit and gazelles.'

Lawrence had grown actively to dislike the Turks, who were masters of Syria, and who treated the Arabs as inferiors. He also disliked the Germans, who were tiresome neighbours at Carchemish, and who were helping to strengthen the grasp of the Turks upon what remained of the Ottoman Empire. Nor did he care for the obvious colonial ambitions of the French in this area. An idea began to attract him: Arabia should be freed from oppressive Turkish rule, and enjoy a large measure of freedom and self-government as a part of the British Empire. Ideas, for Lawrence, always had to be translated into action. So he was ready and willing to be recruited for a survey of the Sinai desert, about which he wrote to his mother: 'We are obviously only meant as red herrings, to give an archaeological colour to a political job.'

Lawrence and Woolley, temporary spies, became for six weeks members of a team led by Captain S. F. Newcombe, mapping the tracks and watering places of Sinai so that the British would be better prepared in the event of war against Turkey. Books were a welcome distraction in the wilderness, and T.E. sent home for some of William Morris's prose romances: *The Well at the World's*

*End, The Glittering Plain, The Sundering Flood,* and *The Wood Beyond the World.* In mid-February, Lawrence left the main party, and went off alone through little-known countryside in the direction of Petra. The Turks had become suspicious of the surveyors – who were ostensibly looking for the route which the Israelites took during their forty years in the desert – and T.E. found that he was being followed by a squad of Turkish soldiers. He led them on a wild scramble, at the end of which he noted with satisfaction: 'I have camped here for two days, and they are still struggling in from all over the compass: the first was ten hours after me: and the last is still missing.'

After a trip along the railway from Maan to Damascus, T.E. returned to Carchemish, where he joined Woolley in saving the Germans from a workers' revolt; and, before the digging season ended, they had some more interesting finds, including a huge head of a god, and the bronze greave of a Hittite soldier. Then, on 10 June, T.E. started back for England.

Eighteen days later Gavril Prinsep, a Serbian conspirator, murdered the Archduke Franz Ferdinand of Habsburg at Sarajevo in Bosnia. The European powers were locked so inescapably in a prison of alliances and obligations that by 4 August one man's murder had led to a European war in which Germany and Austria faced Russia, France and England. It seemed inevitable that the Middle East would be drawn into this conflict. For years, European statesmen had viewed with greedy interest the weakened body of the Ottoman Empire, and the great question in their minds had been: 'Who will control Constantinople when Turkey collapses?' This collapse seemed to have been averted in 1908, when some Ottoman patriots, led by Enver Bey and calling themselves the Young Turks, successfully deposed the Sultan Abdul Hamid, and began a last-ditch attempt to modernize their country. For a while the subject nationalities, including the Arabs, were given a measure of freedom; but then Enver, terrified at the power of the forces which he had let loose, reversed his policy, and became more repressive than the Sultan before him. The Arab deputies were scattered, Arab societies forbidden, and the Arabic language suppressed. There was a Turkish garrison even in the holy city, Mecca, stronghold of Sherif Hussein, the most powerful and independent Arab leader. Many Arabs now thought of revolution, and secret societies sprang up dedicated to liberation from Turkish rule. It remained to be seen whether Turkey's probable involvement in the European war would give these revolutionaries the opportunity for which they waited so patiently.

Woolley and T.E. had enjoyed working with Captain Newcombe for British military intelligence; and when they had finished their

A street scene in Cairo, 1915.

report on the Sinai survey – later published as *The Wilderness of Zin* – they wrote to Newcombe, asking about a war job. He could only put their names on a waiting list. Turkey had now come into the war on the side of Germany and Austria–Hungary. Lawrence, bored and frustrated as he waited at home in Oxford for a message from Newcombe, thought of the future. If, as he hoped, Germany and her allies were defeated, then at the end of the war Russia might install herself at Constantinople, thus gaining access to the Mediterranean for her warships, and threatening the British route to her colonial possessions in the East; while France, as the spoils of any victory, would demand control over Syria. It seemed to Lawrence that only his own idea for Arabian dominions within the Empire would keep the French out of Syria, and help to balance any increase in Russian power. Still there was no sign of a war job; and at last T.E. wrote to Hogarth for help. Hogarth was a member of the Royal Geographical Society and found T.E. a job on the geographical section of the General Staff, drawing a large-scale map of Sinai. T.E.'s knowledge of the Middle East was impressive, and in early December he was sent out to Cairo where, with the rank of second-lieutenant, he became an officer in the new Department of Intelligence in Egypt.

Sherif Hussein of Mecca.

Soon Lawrence was 'in an office all day and every day, adding together scraps of information and writing geographies from memory of little details'. He talked to everyone from whom he could glean information, men like Philip Graves, the *Times* correspondent, who was 'very learned in the Turkish army organisation'. He threw himself wholeheartedly into his work, impressing his colleagues with his quickness and instantaneous grasp of essentials; and he gradually extended the scope of his job until he was acting as an unofficial liaison officer between a number of different government departments.

While agents were recruited, and information was gathered, T.E. and his friends discussed the possibilities of fomenting an Arab revolt against Turkish rule. In March 1915, in an uncensored letter to Hogarth, T.E. wrote of using the Idrisi, a leading Arab family in Mesopotamia, 'to roll up Syria by way of the Hejaz in the name of the Sherif ... and rush right up to Damascus'. He was referring to Sherif Hussein of Mecca, who, since Abdul Hamid had been deposed, was the effective spiritual leader of Islam. The British had promised in 1914 that, in return for Hussein's co-operation, they would help him against foreign aggression and guarantee that no intervention took place in Arabia, but Hussein had refused to commit himself. Now, in early 1915, after the failure of their attempt to cross the Suez Canal into Egypt, the Turks began a repressive internal campaign against Arab cultural and political leaders; and Hussein began a protracted correspondence with Sir Henry McMahon, the British High Commissioner in Egypt, declaring the Arab desire for freedom and unity.

By November 1915, Lawrence had heard of the deaths of two of his brothers. Frank had been killed in France on 9 May, and T.E.'s favourite brother, Will, an observer in the Royal Flying Corps, had died after his aeroplane was shot down. T.E. felt that it was not right for him to go on living safely in Cairo and, though it was some time before he saw active service, he did leave Cairo for a while, on a mission to Mesopotamia.

In Mesopotamia, the Indian army under General Townshend had advanced up the Tigris to Ctesiphon; but by the beginning of 1916 they had been forced back to Kut, where they were soon surrounded by a large Turkish army led by Khalil Pasha. In an attempt to buy off the Turkish General, Aubrey Herbert, a Member of Parliament now attached to Military Intelligence, Cairo, was sent with Colonel Beach and T. E. Lawrence – both of Military Intelligence – to Mesopotamia, with power to offer Khalil up to one million pounds. The mission was a failure; and Townshend, whose troops were living on a daily ration of four ounces of flour with a

General Townshend at Kut with staff of the 6th Division.

little horseflesh, was forced to surrender in company with four other generals, and thirteen thousand officers and men.

Lawrence had got on badly with the army officers at British headquarters. They thought him conceited – after all, he was a very junior officer – and they opposed his plan for raising an Arab rebellion against Turkey. Their idea was that after the war Mesopotamia should be ruled by the British on strictly colonial lines, and they did not want to encourage Arab nationalism. It would have annoyed them greatly to hear of the work of the Arab Bureau in Cairo. Formed early in 1916 by General Clayton, the Bureau was a small Intelligence unit, with the status of an official branch of the Foreign Office. When in the spring of 1916 it began to publish an Intelligence Journal, the *Arab Bulletin*, T.E. was responsible for the early numbers. On behalf of the Bureau, he also interviewed refugees from Syria, showing particular interest in details of the secret societies which were working for Arab liberation. The Turks, fearing the work of these societies, had hanged two groups of leading Arabs by the end of May; and when, soon after this, Hussein heard that a large Turkish force was moving southwards towards Medina, he decided that he must act. On 5 June his eldest son Ali made an unsuccessful attack on Medina; and then on 9 June Hussein himself took up arms.

T.E. was jubilant when he heard of the Revolt. He wrote to his mother to say that, if it succeeded, it would be 'the biggest thing in the Near East since 1550'. After three days Hussein had smoked out and captured the small Turkish force in Mecca, and by September his forces had captured Jedda, Yenbo, Rabegh, Leath, Um Lejj, Kanufdeh, and Taif. For the British, McMahon was put in charge of the political side of the Revolt; military aid was to be directed by Sir Reginald Wingate, Governor of the Sudan; while Colonel Wilson became British representative at Jedda. Lawrence himself hoped to be permanently transferred from Military Intelligence to the Arab Bureau; but Holdich, his new chief, 'didn't like my manners' and was unwilling to allow the move. Asking Clayton and Hogarth to do what they could for him in his absence, T.E. requested leave, and travelled down to Jedda with Sir Ronald Storrs, McMahon's Oriental Secretary, who was to have talks with Hussein's second son, Abdulla.

They enjoyed a calm run down the Red Sea on the *Lama*, a small converted liner: 'By day', T.E. wrote later, 'we lay in shadow; and for great part of the glorious nights we would tramp up and down the wet deck under the stars in the steaming breath of the southern wind. But when at last we anchored in the outer harbour ... then the heat of Arabia came out like a drawn sword, and struck us speechless.' Colonel Wilson sent a launch to

A street scene in Jeddah, photographed by Ronald Storrs in October 1916.

*my first photo. in Hejaz T.E.*

Bringing a 5″ howitzer to Rabegh. T.E.'s own marginal note records this as the first of the many photographs which he took during the Arab Revolt.

meet them; and they went straight to the Consulate. Soon Abdulla rode up on a white mare, with an escort of richly-armed slaves. T.E. noted that Abdulla, though only 35, was putting on weight, and had a friendly and humorous disposition to match. They sat in a circle, and Wilson opened the discussion by reading out a telegram which stated that all British troops were needed on the Egyptian front, and that the few aircraft which had been sent to help the Arabs would be withdrawn. Then they talked about the state of the Arab campaign. The Turks were using the Hejaz railway to collect transport and supplies to reinforce Medina, and had also driven back an army led by Hussein's third son, Feisal. A Turkish mobile column was preparing to advance on Rabegh, and to recapture the coastal areas which Hussein had seized during the first months of the Revolt. As the discussion continued, they touched on the whereabouts of the various Turkish regiments. This was common knowledge in the Arab Bureau, and Storrs later wrote that as Syrian, Anatolian, and other names came up, 'Lawrence at once stated exactly which unit was in which position, until Abdulla turned to me in amazement: "Is this man God, to know everything?"' On the strength of this favourable impression, T.E. secured a letter of introduction to Feisal, so that he could go up-country to see the situation for himself.

During the next two days, Lawrence had several meetings with Ruhi, a Persian agent of Storrs', who compiled for him a list of vernacular Arabic expressions, and gave him detailed information about the customs and habits of the Hejaz Arabs. Then T.E. left by ship for Rabegh, where Sherif Ali was in charge, helped by Zeid, his young half-brother. Ali supplied T.E. with a guide called

Tafas, and a camel. The first stage of the journey would be through the lands of a pro-Turkish tribe, so, to keep the journey a secret, Ali did not let them start until after sunset; and then he gave T.E. an Arab cloak and head-cloth to wrap over his uniform, so that he would present the right silhouette in the dark.

They passed through palm groves, and then out under the stars over flat sand. T.E. was thinking 'how this was the pilgrim road, down which, for uncounted centuries, the people of the north had come to visit the Holy City.... It seemed that the Arab revolt might be in a sense a return pilgrimage.' At times, as the soft plain merged into beds of drift sand, the camels plunged and strained a little, and the saddles creaked; but there was no other variety. Before midnight they halted, and T.E. rolled himself tightly in his cloak, chose a hollow of his own size and shape, and slept in it. They were up again an hour before dawn, and were soon crossing the Wadi Fura, with its thorn trees and low scrub; and so they came to the Masturah well, where they watered the camels. At last they reached the safety of the tribal lands of the Masruh, where Tafas was at home. In the hamlet of Bir el Sheikh, a collection of twenty miserable huts, they shared a dough cake cooked over a brushwood fire. On the morning of the following day, after three more long, exhausting rides, they arrived at the village of Hamra, which was crowded with Feisal's troops. They forded a stream, and went up a walled path between trees to the top of a mound where there was a long, low house. 'Tafas said something to a slave who stood there with silver-hilted sword to hand. He led me to an inner court, on whose further side, framed between the uprights of a black doorway, stood a white figure waiting.' This was Feisal. T.E. calls him a prophet, and he was an inspiring figure, tall and slender in long white silk robes, his brown head-cloth bound with a brilliant scarlet and gold cord. He had seen military service with the Turks, and had been educated by them; but his father Hussein had made sure that he remained a true Arab at heart, ordering him into Arab dress when he returned to the Hejaz, and sending him out into the wilds with Hussein's Camel Corps to patrol the pilgrim roads for months at a time. T.E. made a particular effort to attach himself to Feisal, feeling that he would be more likely than any of his brothers to bring the Arab Revolt to victory.

Feisal explained how the Turkish superiority in heavy guns had made the capture of Medina impossible; the English had only given him four twenty-year-old Krupps, mountain guns with a range of three thousand yards. He wished to build up a mobile force with trained officers who would be a match for the Turkish regular troops. T.E. promised that he would encourage his superiors to set

The Emir Feisal: portrait by Augustus John.

The quay at Yenbo,
photographed by T.E.L.

up a base at Yenbo for stores, supplies, gun-crews and professional army advisers. In the morning, he wandered among Feisal's eight thousand men. He found them in good spirits, especially as Hussein paid not only the fighting men, but their families; but he soon realized that pay was not all that mattered to them: the Turks often gave Arab tribes large sums of money, for which they received no active service.

With a new escort, T.E. began the return journey. At their final camping-place, not far from Yenbo, they lit a fire of aromatic wood, to bake bread and boil coffee, and 'slept sweetly with the salt sea air cool on our chafed faces. We rose at two in the morning, and raced our camels over a featureless plain of hard shingle and wet sand to Yenbo, which stood up with walls and towers on a reef of coral rag.' Four days later, a ship called in to take T.E. back to Jedda. Before leaving, he talked to Nuri es Said, a Bagdadi staff officer who was now second-in-command of the Arab regulars. Nuri repeated Feisal's requests for help and later wrote: 'I never hoped my words would have the effect which they had afterwards. I remember now Lawrence's words when we parted: "I shall do my best to help you, and, God willing, it will be all right. Do not worry."'

From Jedda, T.E. begged a passage to Port Sudan, where he met Joyce and Davenport, two British officers who were about to leave for Rabegh to assist the Arabs. He then went on to Khartoum, where he reported to Sir Reginald Wingate before returning to Cairo. Here he found that Colonel Brémond, head of the French Military Mission to Jedda, was urging an allied landing in the Hejaz, with himself as commander of a mixed brigade of French and English troops. Lawrence, opposing the spread of French influence, and knowing the Arab distrust of foreign troops, wrote a violent memorandum saying that the tribes would scatter if foreigners landed in force. He was now safely installed in the Arab Bureau; and, as the man with the most extensive up-to-date knowledge of the situation in the Hejaz, his views carried weight: Brémond's plan was dropped.

Not long after this his chief, General Clayton, told T.E. to return to Arabia to act as liaison officer with Feisal. T.E. had enjoyed his trip to the Hejaz, but his present life in Cairo did in fact suit his talents very well, and his first reaction was to protest that he was unfit for the job, saying that he hated responsibility, 'and that in all my life objects had been gladder to me than persons, and ideas than objects'. Clayton told him that regular officers had been asked for who might give more professional military advice to Feisal, but that they might be months arriving; in the meantime, it was important that Feisal should be linked to the British, and that his needs should be promptly notified to Egypt.

By the first week in December 1916, T.E. – now with the rank of captain – was back in Yenbo. Here he watched Arabs being trained in the use of dynamite by Garland, a demolition expert

Garland and Colonel Clayton.

31

Captain T. E. Lawrence in the Arab dress which Feisal advised him to wear.

and an officer in the Royal Engineers, who would 'shovel a handful of detonators in his pocket, with a string of primers, fuse and fusees, and jump gaily on his camel for a week's ride to the Hejaz railway'. T.E. heard that Abdulla had taken four thousand men from Mecca to blockade Medina; that Zeid was harrying Turkish communications in the hills; and that Feisal was in Wadi Yenbo. He rode out to find Feisal with Sherif Abd el Kerim. They had heard that the date plantations of Nakhl Mubarak were deserted, but when they reached them they saw 'flame, and the flame-lit smoke of many fires, while the hollow ground re-echoed with the roaring of thousands of excited camels, and volleying of shots or shoutings in the darkness'. Abd el Kerim slipped a cartridge into the breech of his rifle, and went quietly ahead on foot to find out what was happening. He came back half an hour later to report that the troops were part of Feisal's army. Picking their way through his five thousand men to the island of calm where Feisal sat dictating letters, they heard that the Turks had outmanoeuvred Zeid and the hill tribes. Zeid had only just managed to escape. The road to Yenbo was open to the Turks, and Feisal had fallen back to protect his base. Now they were waiting for a Turkish onslaught.

Lawrence found that most of the Arabs took him for a Syrian officer because of his European dress, but he reported that Feisal treated him well, and 'lets me ask, hear and see everything, including his agents'. Feisal soon asked T.E. to wear Arab clothes in camp: they would be more comfortable and less conspicuous. Lawrence agreed; and later many British and French officers followed his example.

For several days there was no Turkish attack, and life in camp followed a simple, unvarying routine. Just before daybreak, the Imam uttered his call to prayer. A few minutes later, a slave brought sweetened coffee to Lawrence. The flap of Feisal's tent was thrown open, inviting household callers; and after the morning's news, a tray of dates was brought in, and Feisal dictated to his secretaries, refreshed by alternate cups of bitter coffee and sweet tea. At about eight o'clock Feisal went to the reception tent, where he dealt with suppliants for most of the day; though there was a break from noon until two o'clock for lunch and private business. In the evening he walked with his friends; and after the sunset prayer he planned the night's patrols. Between six and seven o'clock there was a silent meal, with the beans, lentils, spinach and sweet cakes of lunch, but with cubes of boiled mutton added to the rice tray. Finally there were stories and the singing of tribal poets to listen to; and occasionally Feisal played chess before retiring for the night.

T.E. decided that he would be more useful helping to organize the defence of Yenbo; and from there he telegraphed Captain

Outside Feisal's tent in Nakhl Mubarak; photographed by T.E.L.

Feisal and his army retreating to Yenbo. Lawrence wrote: 'Our war seemed entering its last act. I took my camera, and from the parapet of the Medina gate got a fine photograph of the brothers coming in.'

Boyle of the Royal Navy, who sent five ships to his aid. Zeid also turned up at Yenbo, with eight hundred men; and then news came that there had been a disastrous battle at Nakhl Mubarak. One of the groups of Hejazi tribesmen in Feisal's army, the Juheina, had broken, and Feisal was retreating to Yenbo. 'Our war', T.E. wrote later, 'seemed entering its last act.'

First Feisal and the main army came in; and then the Juheina tribesmen arrived, saying that they had only retired from the fighting for a rest and a cup of coffee. There was no time for recriminations. With Garland as engineer-in-chief, Yenbo was prepared for battle. At eleven o'clock at night, there was an alarm, and the garrison went silently to their places; while Boyle's ships were warned, and their combined searchlights traversed the flat land in complex intersections. Afterwards an Arab guide told Lawrence that he had led an advance party of Turks, who planned to rush Yenbo in the dark and stamp out Feisal's army; 'but their hearts failed them at the silence and the blaze of lighted ships from end to end of the harbour, with the eerie beams of the searchlights revealing the bleakness of the glacis they would have to cross.'

The Turks withdrew to Nakhl Mubarak, where they were bombed by two British seaplanes, and forced to retire to Bir Said. The situation still looked desperate, and T.E. wrote that the Turkish position threatened Feisal's rear and his base: 'his troops are still quite unfit for work, and he estimates it will take him a week to get the Juheina and Northern Harb [another Hejazi tribe] at work again ... [The] situation is hopeful, if the Turks have not got a strong force in Wadi Safra. If they have, we shall have a cataclysm shortly.' For the Turkish commander, Fakhri Pasha, had now begun a slow advance along the Wadi Safra towards Rabegh. This was a more direct route to Mecca, and left Feisal isolated at Yenbo.

Lawrence was now aware of the Sykes–Picot agreement between England, Russia and France, by which at the end of the war France would get most of Syria, in return for British control of Mesopotamia, while Palestine was to be governed by an international régime. All this ran counter to T.E.'s vision of the future; and when he visited Rabegh, he found to his horror that Brémond was hoping not only to land allied troops in the Hejaz, but to calm down the whole Arab Revolt.

On returning to Yenbo, T.E. at once urged that the Arabs should go on to the offensive. By marching north to Wejh, they would extend the threat to the Hejaz railway, and perhaps induce Fakhri to withdraw from his attempt on Mecca. Feisal agreed, and also sent a message to ask his brother Abdulla to move to Wadi Ais, a hundred kilometres north of Medina. From Wadi Ais he could

pose a more direct threat to the Turkish lines of communication along the railway.

A few days later, T.E. took part in his first raid, against a Turkish encampment; and then, on 3 January 1917, he set out with Feisal for Wejh. 'The order of march was splendid and rather barbaric,' he wrote to Colonel Wilson. 'Feisal in front, in white: Sharraf [whom Lawrence later described as 'a powerful man, perhaps the most capable of all the sherifs in the army'] on his right in red headcloth and henna-dyed tunic and cloak; myself on his left in white and red; behind us three banners of purple silk, with gold spikes; behind them three drummers playing a march, and behind them again a wild bouncing mass of 1,200 camels of the bodyguard, all packed as closely as they could move, the men in every variety of coloured clothes, and the camels nearly as brilliant in their trappings, and the whole crowd singing at the tops of their voices a warsong in honour of Feisal and his family.'

Feisal had suggested taking enough men from different tribes to show that the Revolt was to be above tribal rivalries and vendettas. On the march Abd el Kerim surveyed the camp-fires of the scattered contingents, and said to Lawrence, half proudly and half sadly: 'We are no longer Arabs, but a people.'

On 16 January, the army entered Um Lejj, a group of three small villages on a plain under red granite hills. T.E. wrote from here that Feisal 'is charming towards me, and we get on perfectly.' Arab historians, groaning perhaps under the injustice of being helped by a foreigner during a war of liberation, have written slightingly about

Some of the enemy whom Lawrence faced, including **Fakhri-ed-Din Pasha, Ibn Rashid, and Ibn Rashid's standard-bearer.**

Feisal with an Ageyl bodyguard
setting out for Wejh on 3
January 1917; photographed by
T.E.L.

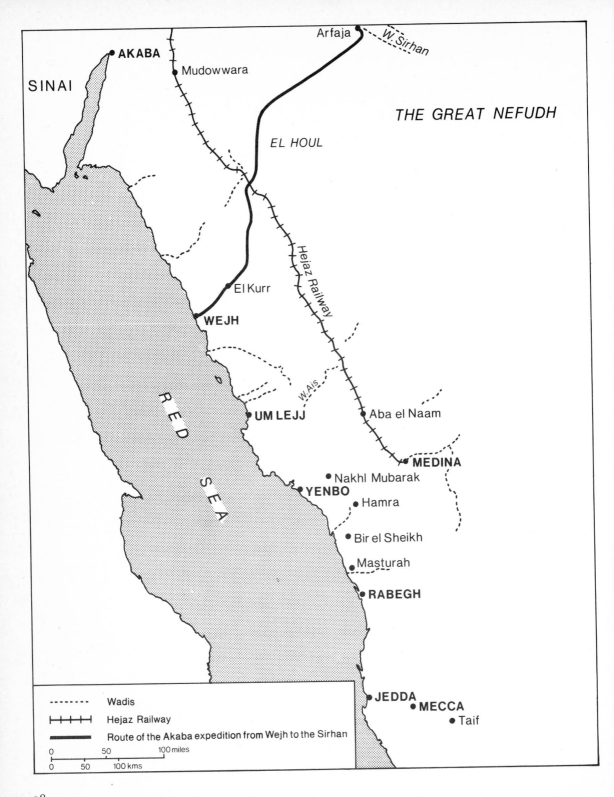

SINAI

AKABA

Mudowwara

Arfaja

W. Sirhan

THE GREAT NEFUDH

EL HOUL

El Kurr

WEJH

Hejaz Railway

R E D    S E A

W. Ais

UM LEJJ

Aba el Naam

MEDINA

Nakhl Mubarak

YENBO

Hamra

Bir el Sheikh

Masturah

RABEGH

JEDDA

MECCA

Taif

- - - - - - - -   Wadis

├┼┼┼┼┤   Hejaz Railway

━━━━━   Route of the Akaba expedition from Wejh to the Sirhan

| 0 | 50 | 100 miles |
| 0 | 50 | 100 kms |

Lawrence's position in Feisal's entourage. They say, for example, that it was enough for him 'to hear a conversation, familiarise himself with the decisions made, and perhaps make a few remarks himself, to claim at the end of the war that he was the man who directed the Revolt'. In his official capacity, of course, T.E. was merely a liaison officer. But it is clear from many accounts that, as he won the confidence and respect of the Arab leaders, so he began to take an active part in guiding and directing Arab policy. Colonel Joyce later recalled that, at the first Arab Council he attended at which T.E. was present, T.E. rarely spoke until all the opposing arguments had ended in smoke, and 'he then dictated his plan of action, which was usually adopted, and everyone went away satisfied.'

The decision to move north had certainly proved correct. The Turkish army had continued its march on Rabegh for some days, but each day lost some forty camels and twenty men killed or wounded by Arab marksmen in the hills. News of Feisal's advance decided Fakhri on returning to Medina. Most of his troops settled down to hold a passive defence of the trenches round the city; while strong garrisons were posted at all the water-holes between Medina and Tebuk, with smaller garrisons between them, and daily patrols along the track.

Feisal's army was delayed by heavy rain, and by the time he reached Wejh on 25 January, it had been captured by Captain Boyle

*Opposite*
The Hejaz campaign.

Emir Feisal's army during a review at Wejh in January 1917; photographed by T.E.L.

and some Arab irregulars. Now all the Hejazi coast bar the small towns of Dhaba and Muweilah was in Arab hands. T.E. travelled to Egypt to report to his superiors, and discovered that Brémond had yet another scheme for an allied expedition, this time to capture Akaba, the only Turkish port in the Red Sea. Feeling that that this was part of the French plan to confine the Arab Revolt to southern Arabia, T.E. outmanoeuvred Brémond by persuading Feisal to reject the scheme. By the end of January, T.E., Feisal, and Captain Newcombe were themselves planning an attack on Akaba: an attack by the Arabs, from inland. Newcombe later wrote that this plan was 'entirely conceived by Lawrence, who was its real leader and animating spirit'.

For the moment, there was other work to be done. Garland and Newcombe were picking holes in the Hejaz railway with high explosives, while Feisal was winning over the northern tribes. The coastal Howeitat had joined the Revolt, and now the tribes owing obedience to Nuri Shaalan came in. Nuri's favour was necessary to travel the Sirhan, a desert roadway which led from Jauf to Azrak, and would enable Feisal to link up with the Eastern Howeitat, and their chief Auda abu Tayi. Feisal swore tribal leaders on the Koran 'to wait while he waited, march while he marched, to yield obedience to no Turk, to deal kindly with all who spoke Arabic, and to put independence above life, family and goods'.

In the first week of March, Clayton informed Lawrence that the Turks had ordered Fakhri to withdraw from Medina: but that the British did not welcome the prospect of another twenty-five thousand Turkish troops in Sinai. Feisal agreed to put the British interests first, and wrote to Abdulla, telling him of the urgency of acting against the railway line, to prevent the Turks from leaving Medina. Before setting out to take the letter to Abdulla, T.E. wrote to Colonel Wilson: 'If only we can hold them up for ten days. I'm afraid it will be touch and go.'

Lt. Col. S. F. Newcombe and camel, photographed by T.E.L. in March 1917.

Representatives of tribes coming in under a white flag to swear allegiance to Feisal.

40

On the march, Lawrence was accompanied by a mixed body of Arabs and Moroccans. He suffered a bad attack of dysentery, and ran a heavy fever. While he was ill, his men quarrelled; and then Hamed the Moor shot one of the Ageyl and killed him. To avoid a blood feud, it was necessary for T.E. to dispense summary justice: justice which T.E. later wrote that civilized man would 'shun like the plague if he had not the needy to serve him as hangmen for wages'. After giving Hamed a few moments' delay, T.E. shot him through the chest. 'He fell down on the weeds shrieking, with the blood coming out in spurts over his clothes, and jerked about till he rolled nearly to where I was ... I fired again.' It was a deeply shocking experience.

Ali ibn Hussein (left) and his brother Abdulla (centre).

Captain Hornby, photographed by T.E.L.

At Abdulla's camp in Wadi Ais, T.E. met with a rather chilly reception. This was due partly to the presence of Captain Rahu, a member of the French Military Mission who knew of the differences between Lawrence and Brémond, with whom he was in constant touch; and partly to Abdulla's feeling that T.E. was interfering in things that were no concern of his. Abdulla argued that the Arabs would get independence in the Hejaz after the war in any case, so there was no point in sacrificing Arab lives in the meantime. T.E. found that Abdulla spent his day reading newspapers, eating, sleeping, and teasing a certain Mohammed Hassan, who was set on fire, stoned with pebbles, and stabbed with thorns by Abdulla and his friends. T.E. wrote to his superiors: 'I cannot explain on paper why so little has been done hitherto. Do you remember what Nero did when Rome was burning?' But Abdulla did realize that he must do something positive in return for British gold and weapons; so, while T.E. lay ill, he sent out a force which blew up a locomotive and destroyed eleven kilometres of track.

A month before this, T.E. had written that the Arabs 'hate the Turks, but don't want to obey anyone's orders, and in consequence they turn out only as a mob of snipers or guerrilla fighters ... In their smallness of number ... lies a good deal of their strength, for they are perhaps the most elusive enemy an army ever had.' Now, during his illness, he had time to elaborate his ideas into a theory. He realized that the Turks could defend Arabia indefinitely against the Arabs if they fought regular battles. But 'suppose we were (as we might be) an influence, an idea, a thing intangible, invulnerable, without front or back, drifting about like a gas?' Their aim should be to destroy Turkish bridges, rails, guns, and so on, while keeping Arab casualties to a minimum, and fighting a war in which 'we were to contain the enemy by the silent threat of a vast unknown desert.'

When he was well again, T.E. asked Abdulla to launch a fresh attack on the railway. Sherif Shakir, Abdulla's cousin and second in command, was enthusiastic; he was put in command of an attack on Aba el Naam station, and Lawrence and Captain Rahu were allowed to join him. There was a train halted in the station when they arrived, and it was decided to mine the railway to the north and south, with an artillery attack on the station itself. T.E. helped to lay one of the mines, which was a trigger action to fire into twenty pounds of blasting gelatine when the weight of the locomotive overhead deflected the rails. He arrived back to join the main party 'just as the guns opened fire. They did excellently, and crashed in all the top of one building, damaged the second, hit the pump-room, and holed the water-tank. One lucky shell caught the front waggon of the train in the siding, and it took fire furiously.'

A portrait of Auda abu Tayi of the Howeitat, by Eric Kennington. Lawrence grew to admire Auda, and wrote of him: 'He saw life as a saga. All the events in it were significant: all personages in contact with him, heroic.'

The train reversed out of the station towards T.E.'s mine; but the charge exploded late, and the train, only slightly damaged, managed to escape. The Arabs then wiped out one Turkish outpost and captured another, before retiring with only one of their own men slightly hurt. This raid, and others which followed it, had the desired effect: the Turks abandoned their attempt to evacuate Medina.

Lawrence travelled back to Wejh in the second week of April, and reported to Feisal. All seemed to be going well. More cars had arrived from Egypt, and stores and soldiers were being moved up from Yenbo and Rabegh. Newcombe and Hornby were 'tearing at the railway day and night'; and Feisal was making good progress with the tribes. T.E. was about to take his leave when Auda abu Tayi of the Howeitat arrived. T.E. soon grew to like this 'tall, strong figure, with a bearded face, passionate and tragic ... He had come down to us like a knight-errant, chafing at our delay in Wejh,

Sherif Nasir (sitting in right foreground), photographed by T.E.L.

anxious only to be acquiring merit for Arab freedom in his own lands.'

In T.E.'s absence, opinion had swung in favour of two plans which he strongly opposed: a full-scale attack on Medina, and a British attempt on Akaba from the sea. The attack on Medina never happened; but a unit of British marines, covered by naval guns, did force the Turkish garrison at Akaba to withdraw. But the Turks simply took up strong positions in the hills immediately over-looking the town, and the marines, unable to advance or to remain, were forced to depart. Not long after this Lieutenant-Colonel Sir Mark Sykes – the English half of the Sykes–Picot agreement – looked in at Wejh, in a visit which brought home to T.E. the likeli-hood that promises made to the Arabs would be broken at the end of the war. He later wrote: 'I tried to make the crime of so exploiting the blood and hope of another people as small in degree as it was necessary in kind'; and the only way in which he could now reconcile his duty to his country, and his own pledges to the Arab leaders, was to push their Revolt ahead as fast and as far as possible.

Auda and Feisal worked out with Lawrence a plan by which a small expedition was to march across two hundred miles of dry and difficult country to the spring pastures of the Howeitat in the Syrian desert. Here they would raise a mobile camel force, and rush Akaba from the east. The leaders of the expedition were to be Sherif Nasir – representing Feisal – Auda abu Tayi, and his kins-man Nesib el Bekri. T.E. was to accompany them, and they were to have an escort of thirty-five of the Ageyl. T.E. wrote in his pocket diary that 'Feisal gave me £1000 Sherif's money as secure fund for expedition'; and it is probable that by 9 May when they set out, he had persuaded him to make this up to more than twenty times that amount. They also took with them fifty-nine pounds of flour per man, a little spare ammunition, a few extra rifles, and six camels loaded with blasting gelatine.

They travelled first to the oasis of Kurr; and on the way Nasir talked to T.E. about his house in Medina, where the Turks were chopping down his palms and fruit trees, where the great well, which had sounded with the creak of bullock-wheels for six hundred years, had fallen silent; and where the garden was becoming as barren as the hills over which they now rode. On the treacherous paths beyond Kurr they lost two camels: the Arabs killed them where they lay broken, cut them up, and shared them out as meat. T.E. was ill again, with boils and fever; and, feeling the burden of his responsibility to the Arabs, he wrote in his pocket diary on the 13th: 'The weight is bearing me down now. Auda last night, +pain+agony today.'

One afternoon, resting in a peaceful valley, Lawrence was disturbed by a young Ageyli boy, Daud, asking him to intercede for his friend and love-fellow Farraj, who had burned their tent as a practical joke, and was going to be beaten by Saad, one of the Ageyli captains. T.E.–who in his time had carried out several practical jokes, including keeping Woolley awake at Carchemish by

Kalaat Sebail at Wejh, 9 May 1917; the party on the day before it started for Sirhan, photographed by T.E.L.

Farraj and Daud.

cutting a wind-vane from a biscuit tin and fixing it to his tent pole so that it made a grinding screech all night long – put in a word for Farraj, and Saad allowed Daud to share his friend's sentence. The next morning, while Lawrence and Auda talked of the march ahead, and Nasir flicked sputtering matches across the tent at them, the two bent figures of Farraj and Daud hobbled up, with pain in their eyes, and asked to be taken on as T.E.'s servants. When T.E. said that he was a simple man who disliked servants about him, Daud sulked; but Farraj persisted, kneeling in mute appeal to Nasir. In the end, on Nasir's advice, and because they looked so young and clean, T.E. agreed to take them both.

The expedition continued along the deep gorge of Wadi Jizil, where tamarisk sprouted from a bed of drifted sand, and they met Hornby returning from a raid on the railway. They went on over ruined sandstone land, and then climbed up higher on to volcanic blue-black rock over which the camels picked their way with difficulty. T.E. wrote later: 'Nothing in the march was normal or re-assuring. We felt we were in an ominous land, incapable of life, hostile even to the passing of life, except painfully along such sparse roads as time had laid across its face.' Beyond the lava flats they came to Wadi Diraa, where a deserted camp with empty sardine tins showed that Newcombe and Hornby had been there. The camels were now suffering from mange, but there was no thought of turning back. The small expedition crossed the Hejaz railway on 19 May, and continued north-east over the desolate plain of El Houl. T.E. noted on the back of a message pad: 'Hejaz sun does not scorch but slowly blackens and consumes anything – men to stone – subject to it.'

Now they were tormented by sandstorms, and by a hot breathless wind, so dry that it burned their skin and cracked it; and Auda set watches through the night: for they were in the line of raiding parties, and at night there were no friends in Arabia. They rode slowly down the beds of the Seil Abu Arad and the Wadi Fejr, where they found a well; and then for a short distance the country looked greener, and their hunters killed two gazelles.

From Wadi Fejr, which they reached on 21 May, they steered for the wells of Arfaja in the Sirhan; and passed by a corner of the Great Nefudh, the famous belts of sand-dune which Gertrude Bell and other travellers had crossed. There was more sand, and then polished mud underfoot. The sandstorms continued, and by the evening of the 23rd they had run out of water, and some of the camels were being led by hand in case they collapsed from exhaustion.

At midday on the 24th, halfway across the scorched plain of the Bisaita, T.E. discovered that one of his Ageyl, Gasim, was missing: though his camel was with them, fully laden. By desert practice, he was responsible for the life of his follower; and, feeling furious with Gasim, he turned his camel round and went back alone to search for him. Nearly two hours later, he saw something black ahead of him: it was Gasim, half-crazed by the sun. T.E. lifted him up on to his camel, swore that unless he stopped moaning about his thirst he would throw him off again, and turned back after the caravan. He still might have lost his way; but Auda, complaining bitterly about Lawrence risking his life for 'that thing', came back with two of Nasir's men, and found him.

In the evening they reached the Kasseim of Sirhan, sandhills coated with tamarisk. There was still no water, but after five days across the blazing Houl in the teeth of sandstorms, the Sirhan seemed beautiful; and on the following morning they came to the wells of Arfaja, and quenched their thirst. Then they drank coffee, and talked about the goal of their efforts: Akaba, and freedom for the Arabs. By 27 May they had reached the camping grounds of the Howeitat, and their dangerous desert crossing was over.

Auda rode off to visit Nuri Shaalan, who controlled the Sirhan area, to give him a present of money, and to ask him to keep their presence in the desert a secret from the Turks. While he was away, the Howeitat and the rest of the group moved gently northwards towards Nebk, which was to be the rallying-place of the tribes. Howeitat hospitality was boundless, and each day T.E. and his companions were feasted twice. After politely pretending not to hear their host calling them to eat, they would turn and find a huge bowl piled high with rice and mutton. The bowl was the largest in the tribe, a magnificent piece of copper, five feet across, inscribed in Arabic: 'To the glory of God, and in trust of mercy at the last, the property of His poor suppliant, Auda abu Tayi'. After a first sitting of more than twenty men, there were second and third sittings; and finally the children and dogs were left to gnaw at the bones.

Auda returned after an apparently successful visit to Nuri Shaalan, and then they arrived at Nebk, and began to enrol men. Many of the Arabs now wanted to gather a large force, and march immediately upon Damascus; but T.E. persuaded Auda and Nasir that they were being over-enthusiastic. They might capture Damascus, but without support they could not hope to hold it for long. Akaba must remain their goal for the present.

The long ride over dangerous country with Auda and Nasir had brought T.E. much closer to the Arabs: had, in his own words, made companions of their minds. Part of him was caught up in their

Auda abu Tayi and Sherif Nasir, photographed by T.E.L.

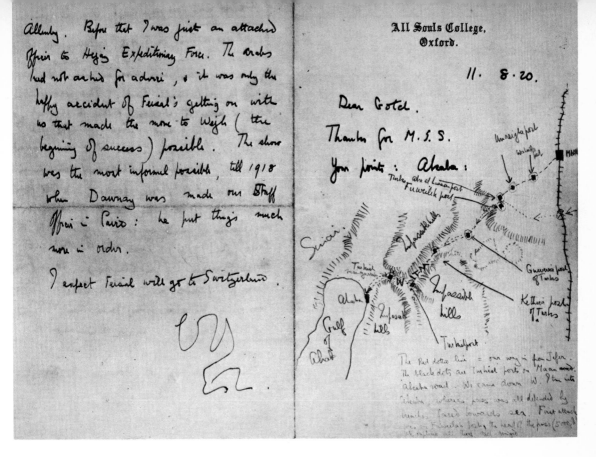

T. E. Lawrence's own diagram of the Akaba campaign, sent from All Souls to Leonard Gotch, a former map officer at Cairo, who wished to lecture about T.E.'s exploits.

wild enthusiasm for freedom; but another part of him felt guilty and ashamed about his role, as the representative of a country which planned to break its promises. In a state of depression, he wrote in his pocket diary on 5 June: 'Can't stand another day here. Will ride N. & chuck it'; and he drafted a message to Clayton, which he then pencilled out again, telling that he was going off to Damascus, hoping to get killed on the way, adding: 'We are calling them to fight for us on a lie, and I can't stand it.' He did ride off into Syria with two companions on a reconnaissance trip, to study key positions for future campaigns, and to contact the more important of Feisal's secret friends. He rode hard: his pocket diary shows that he had ridden one camel to the point of collapse within four days of setting out. But, although he went as far as Damascus, he achieved less than he hoped (for example, his entry on the 13th reads: 'wanted to see M but He – could not'); and, to protect those whom he did contact, he later shrouded the trip in mystery, telling Robert Graves in 1927 to write: 'nothing certain is known of his purpose, his route, and the results of his journey.' However, he returned to Nebk on 18 June, and wrote a full report of his trip for Clayton; and he was now in better spirits again, feeling perhaps that fate was on his side after all.

Nasir and Auda had now recruited a force more than five hundred strong. They had fresh camels, but money and food were running out, so there was no point in further delay. On 19 June they set out on the road to Akaba, planning to travel through Bair, El Jefer, and Aba el Lissan, only sixteen miles from the Turkish stronghold at Maan. The Turks had now heard of an Arab army in the desert, and, to protect Maan, they began dynamiting all the nearby wells. When the Arabs reached Bair, they seemed to be just too late: smoke still hung in the air around the Bair wells. But the Turks had done their demolition work badly: thirty pounds of gelignite had failed to explode in one of the wells, and the Arabs were able to repair it.

In order to draw the Turks away from this area, a fifth of the expedition, including Lawrence, and led by Auda's nephew Zaal, left Bair to carry out a raid. They blew up some rails in the Minifir area, and attacked the two stone houses of Atwi station, destroying one of them, blowing up some rails, cutting the telegraph, and even driving off a flock of twenty-four sheep. After feasting on the sheep they re-entered Bair, successful, and without a single casualty. News soon came that the Turks were hunting for them near Nebk. Believing that the wells at Bair and El Jefer were destroyed, they had no fears about an attack from that quarter.

But at El Jefer too, the Turks had failed to block the wells completely. When the Arabs arrived there, they found one well whose shaft was intact: the upper stones had merely clapped together over its mouth, and it was speedily re-opened. Now men of the Dhumaniyeh tribe were sent forward to attack Fuweilah, the blockhouse which covered the head of the pass of Aba el Lissan, and controlled the road from Maan to Akaba. The first attack of the Dhumaniyeh was beaten off; but the Turkish garrison miscalculated badly when they made a sortie against the nearest Arab encampment, murdering an old man, six women, and seven children. The Dhumaniyeh, in their fury, cut off the Turks on their return, captured the fort, and killed nearly the whole garrison.

On hearing of this success the main Arab army mounted and rode for Ghadir el Haj, the first railway station south of Maan; while a smaller group rode to the north of Maan, to create a diversion by threatening the herds of Turkish camels which were pastured there. At Ghadir, the garrison was soon driven off, and ten bridges and many rails destroyed; but then the Dhumaniyeh arrived with unwelcome news. The Turkish survivors from Fuweilah had reached Maan just as a relief battalion was arriving; and this battalion had set out straight away as a punitive column. They had found the blockhouse deserted, except for the vultures flying above it; and their battalion commander, not wishing to alarm his young troops with the sight of the Turkish dead, had not entered the blockhouse, but encamped by the roadside spring in the Aba el Lissan valley. Unless these Turks could be dislodged from the pass, there would be no hope of riding down the road to Akaba. The Arab army set out immediately.

While the Turks were still sleeping in the valley, the Arabs surrounded them, and soon after dawn began sniping steadily at them from the hilltops. The Turks quickly found cover under the slopes and rock faces by the water; while the Arabs grew hot and thirsty under a sun so fierce that rifles seared their hands, and even some of the toughest warriors were overcome by the heat and had to be carried into the shade to recover. At last, soon after noon, Auda and fifty horsemen, shooting from the saddle, charged against the Turkish rear, and broke them. Then Nasir and four hundred camel men charged them in the flank. It was a wild charge, and T.E., in the thick of it, was unlucky enough to fire his fifth shot through the skull of his own camel. The camel fell instantly. Expecting to be trampled to death, T.E. found verses of a poem running through his head:

> For Lord I was free of all thy flowers,
>     but I chose the world's sad roses,
> And that is why my feet are torn
>     and mine eyes are blind with sweat.

But the camel's body lay behind him like a rock, dividing the charge into two streams, and he survived. The attack had been a success; the Arabs took 160 prisoners, while more than 300 dead and dying Turks were scattered over the open valleys. Their own losses were no more than a handful of men killed. For the *Arab Bulletin*, T.E. wrote: 'Auda himself (in front, of course) had a narrow escape, since two bullets smashed his field glasses, one pierced his revolver holster, three struck his sheathed sword, and his horse was killed under him. He was wildly pleased with the whole affair.'

After their victory, the Howeitat wanted to attack Maan; Nasir and Auda let them go to capture nearby Mreigha and Waheida, but Lawrence convinced them all that the important objective was Akaba, whose capture would re-open sea contact with Suez, and lead to a proper supply of food, money, guns and ammunition. That night, after wearying hours of persuasion among the restless, noisy Arabs, T.E. wandered to where the Turkish corpses lay in heaps on the battle-ground. Many of them were as young as his brothers who had already died in the War; and, pitying them, he straightened their limbs, 'half longing to be one of those quiet ones, not of the . . . mob up the valley . . . with death, whether we won or lost, waiting to end the history'.

*(Above)* Wadi Itm near
Resafl, where the terms of the
Turkish surrender were discussed
on 5 July 1917; photographed by
T.E.L.

*(Far left)* T.E.'s photograph of
the triumphal entry into Akaba.

*(Left)* T. E. Lawrence at Akaba
on one of his camels. John
Graves writes that his brother
Philip 'once saw T.E. mount his
racing camel at speed.... He
sprinted behind the camel, took a
flying leap, and landed with his
left foot on its left hock. As its
right leg swung forward, he
placed his right foot on the right
hock. At the same time he seized
the camel's tail and hauled
himself up into the saddle.'

Next day, the Arab army travelled to Guweira, where the local Sheikh, Ibn Jad, had heard of their success and promptly taken prisoner the Turkish garrison. The next defended post, Kethira, refused to parley; and Ibn Jad and his men were ordered to prove their loyalty to the Arab cause by attacking it. This they did, helped by an eclipse of the moon which meant that the superstitious Turks, instead of defending the post, were firing rifles and clanging copper pots to rescue the threatened satellite.

Travelling down the narrows of Wadi Itm on 5 July, they found Turkish post after Turkish post abandoned. The Turks had withdrawn into Khedra, the entrenched position which covered Akaba, but whose defences were all built facing the sea. By the afternoon the Arabs were in contact with the main Turkish position, and the next morning the Turks surrendered gladly, 'holding up their arms and crying "Muslim Muslim" as soon as they saw us'. The Arabs raced the last four miles to Akaba, through a driving sandstorm, and splashed triumphantly into the sea. Two months after Nasir, Auda, Nesib and Lawrence had set out from Wejh with thirty-five Ageyl, Akaba was taken.

Leaving Auda and Nasir to defend Akaba, T.E. took a small body of men and rode across the desert to the British post at Shatt, opposite Suez on the eastern side of the Canal. Shatt had been evacuated after an outbreak of plague, and when Lawrence telephoned Suez HQ, they told him to get in touch with Inland Water Transport, whose job it was to ferry people across the Canal. Inland Water Transport informed T.E. that they had no free boats, but that they would send one in the morning to take him to the quarantine department. Then they rang off. When he rang them again, and made angry protests, they again rang off; but, just as T.E. was growing 'very vivid', a sympathetic telephone operator intervened, telling him: 'It's no bluidy good, sir, talking to them fookin water boogers.' The operator put him through to the Embarkation Office, who sent a launch to pick him up at once. On the following day, he travelled up to Cairo by train. On the journey he revenged himself upon bureaucracy, by failing to show the military police his special pass. When they tried to interrogate this seeming Arab, in white silk robes, gold head rope and dagger, he told them in fluent English that he was a staff officer in the Meccan army. When they exclaimed that they had never heard of the Meccan army, and didn't know the uniform, his only reply was: 'Would you recognise a Montenegrin dragoon?'

In Cairo, Lawrence reported to Clayton, and the steamer *Dufferin* was immediately sent to Akaba with food, and £16,000 in gold for Nasir to pay the Arab army. Still in his Arab clothes, T.E. was interviewed by Allenby, the new British commander-in-chief. Allenby was impressed by Lawrence, later writing that 'his high forehead

Sir Reginald Wingate and Allenby.

and a clear eye betokened a brain of unusual power, a mind dominant over the body.' He accepted T.E.'s view of the importance of the Arab Revolt in the fight against the Turks, and promised that he would do what he could to help. T.E. then went back to Clayton, and asked to be given real command over operations in Arabia; but, although he was now promoted to the rank of major, his request was turned down, and Colonel Joyce was made commanding officer at Akaba. Joyce was a solid, dependable soldier, and continued to give T.E. a very free rein: a situation which exactly suited T.E.'s temperament and abilities.

Lawrence now suggested to Clayton that the base at Wejh should be closed down, and that Feisal's army should come to Akaba. Feisal would become an army commander under Allenby, and the Arab army would act as Allenby's right wing on his future advance into

Jaafar Pasha, Feisal, and Lt. Col. Joyce (seated, left to right).

Palestine. Lawrence was sent to discuss this with Feisal, who agreed to the idea, ordering his camel corps to proceed at once to Akaba. The regular Arab troops, which had been commanded by Feisal's chief of staff, Jaafar Pasha, since mid-June, were ferried up in the *Hardinge*. T.E. also met Hussein at Jedda, and found him clever and likeable, but knowing little. After the war, he and his sons would need help. 'I do hope we play them fair.'

While he was at Jedda, telegrams from Egypt suggested that the Howeitat were talking terms with the Turks, and that Auda was implicated. Within three days, T.E. was back at Akaba. Out at Guweira, he found Auda, Zaal, and Mohammed el Dheilan. They were angry that the British had not yet sent them a proper reward for the capture of Akaba, and they had indeed been negotiating with the Turks. Lawrence told them that Allenby was about to send them help; and that Feisal himself was on his way to reward them. They were satisfied by these assurances, and T.E. reported to Cairo that there had been no treachery. Incidents like this one, in which he had to help the Arabs in spite of themselves, were exhausting and irritating, and at times T.E. felt like having nothing more to do with them, writing that his task was like 'making bricks without straw or mud.'

During August, there were raids on the Turkish positions near Maan, and some aeroplanes bombed the town as well. Lawrence, who had now learned how to explode mines with the use of a detonator, decided on an attack upon Mudowwara station, eighty

HMS *Humber* at Akaba,
showing Chatham pier;
photographed by T.E.L.

Operations on a fuse,
and interested spectators.

A still from David Lean's film *Lawrence of Arabia*, showing Arabs looting a Turkish train.

miles south of Maan. Several of the tribes had fallen out with each other, so when the expedition set out on 16 September, they had only a little over a hundred men, instead of nearly three hundred. The blind Sherif Aid was the nominal leader, and Zaal came with some of the Dhumaniyeh; but the task of keeping them together fell upon T.E. They found Mudowwara too strongly defended, and so marched south until they came to an ideal place for mine-laying, and an ambush, a point where the railway left the plain, and curved into low hills. At noon, a patrol of a hundred Turks began marching in their direction from the station, and they prepared to move out; but then a train was spotted in the distance. It overtook the patrol, and steamed up into the trap. At a signal from Lawrence, a mine was exploded. 'There followed a terrific roar, and the line vanished from sight beneath a spouting column of black dust and smoke a hundred feet high and wide.' The train was blown up, and most of the Turks in it were killed by machine-gun and mortar fire. The Arabs looted the train, and then made off. For a few anxious moments, T.E. and two sergeants from the base at Akaba found themselves left alone, close to the wrecked train; but then Zaal and another Arab returned to rescue them, and they all went triumphantly home. A few days later, T.E. wrote to a friend. Much of his letter was in a bantering tone, but he added: '—nerves going and temper wearing thin, and one wants an unlimited amount of both...on a show so narrow and voracious as this one loses one's past and one's balance... The killing and killing of Turks is horrible. When you charge in at the finish and find them all over the place in bits, and still alive many of them...'

Meanwhile, volunteers had been recruited from various army units to reinforce Akaba, and among them was Sergeant Tom Beaumont, a qualified gunner for the .303 Vickers, who steamed to Akaba with a cargo of armoured cars. He wrote a private account of his experiences in 1936:

'Shouts, cheers & firing came from the beach; Arabs were dancing in frenzy at the sight of these armoured cars. Bullets began to whistle over our heads, a queer kind of welcome I thought... Soon we had camp pitched near the entrance to Wadi Itm. It was a very narrow pass with rocks and soft sand to add great obstruction to the cars.'

They had months of hard work making a road on which the cars could travel. The heat was so intense that they could not start work until four or five in the afternoon; progress was slow, the days seemed long, and everyone intolerable. But then, one night, as Beaumont was doing sentry-duty, Lawrence came out of the darkness, kindly and confident, with a bodyguard of thirty Arabs: 'Ssh!

(*Above*) T. W. Beaumont after two months' service, on his first weekend pass in January 1916.

(*Left*) Junction of the Wadi Rumm with the Akaba–Guweira road, looking north.

Don't wake the boys. It's quite alright. I'm Lawrence.' He spoke to the officer, and then, before leaving, he leaned down from his camel and asked Beaumont's name. 'I told him, & he said right, see you again before long. Good night sentry . . . I felt inspired, I felt that after all we had a leader to be relied on.' Another Englishman, a mechanic, wrote: 'here was a power who seemed to command one's very soul, of charming persuasive manner, to seduce one's rebellion and counteract all obstinate ideas . . .' .

In the next four months, parties from Akaba destroyed seventeen locomotives. Rumours about Lawrence spread through the desert, and filtered back to the bazaars of Cairo, where Storrs found that 'merchants like Abdala Kahlal, trading with Arabs . . . congratulated me, and enquired after "al-Urenz".' The Turks launched one major counter-attack in the Akaba direction, but were led into a trap by the Arab commander Maulud, and repulsed with heavy losses.

In October, Allenby was making plans to attack the Turkish lines of defence which ran from Gaza to Beersheba. T.E., hoping that the Arabs might contribute something decisive to the campaign, planned to cut one of the bridges in the Yarmuk valley, over which the railway from Palestine climbed on its way to Damascus. This would isolate the Turkish army from its base, and cut off its retreat. Allenby approved the plan, asking for the bridge to be blown up at the end of the first week in November.

Lawrence decided that Azrak should be the base for his attack on the bridges; and he collected a small force, including twelve of his own retinue, some Indian machine-gunners, Ali ibn el Hussein, a Harith Sherif who knew something of Syria; Captain Wood, the base engineer at Akaba, and Emir Abd el Kader, a Damascene of Algerian origins whom Feisal thought to be honest, but who Brémond warned was a spy in the pay of the Turks. By 28 October they had crossed the railway between Ghadir and Shedia, and were south-west of the wells of Jefer, where they found Auda encamped: his Howeitat tribesmen were in dispute over tribal wages, and he only had fifteen men with him. Luckily for him, T.E. was able to settle the dispute. The next morning, after Auda had reinforced Brémond's warning about Abd el Kader, T.E. and his party went on over the Jefer plains. Some of them were new to desert riding, so they proceeded at a gentle pace. T.E. later recalled that 'the golden weather of misty dawns, mild sunlight and evening chill added a strange peacefulness of nature to the peacefulness of our march. This week was a St Martin's summer, which passed like a remembered dream. I felt only that it was very gentle, very comfortable, that the air was happy, and my friends content.'

At Bair they were welcomed by Mifleh, chief of the Beni Sakhr, who joined them with fifteen of his best men. When they rode

from Wadi Bair, Lawrence spent his time less peacefully, listening to the Beni Sakhr, and winning their trust. 'There was nothing so wearing,' he wrote, 'yet nothing so important for the success of my purpose, as this constant mental gymnastic of apparent omniscience at each time of meeting a new tribe.' On 2 November, half a march from Azrak, they met the fighting men of the Serhan tribe, on their way to join Feisal, and persuaded them to turn back with them; and they came to Azrak itself, a blue fort on its rock above the rustling palms. T.E. found Azrak magically haunted, its unfathomable silence 'steeped in the knowledge of wandering poets, champions, lost kingdoms, all the crime and chivalry and dead magnificence of Hira and Ghassas'.

Abd el Kader now deserted them; but they decided to press on, and, reinforced by the Serahin, they crossed the railway line and rode to Abya, where they rested on 6 November. Lawrence and Sherif Ali decided that the final raid should be made by a party of seventy men. The Beni Sakhr under Fahad would be the storming party, while some Serahin guarded the camels, and others carried the blasting gelatine. They set out at sunset, and reached Tell el Shehab and the railway; but someone dropped a rifle and alerted a sentry, who spotted the machine-gunners climbing to a new position. Firing broke out, and then the Serahin porters, frightened of

The first and biggest girder bridge in the Yarmuk valley; the one T.E. attacked on 7 November 1917, but failed to destroy when the blasting gelatine was thrown away.

being blown to pieces, dumped their sacks of gelatine over the edge of the ravine and fled. The attack was thus a complete failure, although before they returned to Azrak they blew up a train near Minifir and captured sixty or seventy rifles. However, the country was now sodden with rain, and it seemed unlikely that Allenby would be able to make a great advance that year.

The stone walls and floors of Azrak were cold and damp: when dogs howled, the Arabs talked of ghosts, and it seemed to T.E. that past and present flowed over them like an uneddying river. Visitors such as Talal el Hareidhin, Sheikh of Tafas, came in from all around, and Sherif Ali recruited them to Feisal's cause.

When the weather cleared a little, T.E. decided to reconnoitre the Deraa area. He set out with three companions, including an old peasant, Faris, with whom he actually entered Deraa. First they examined the station, and then began walking down the east front of the defences. Ignored by groups of Turkish soldiers, they passed by the aerodrome on the way to the town centre. 'There were old Albatross machines in the sheds', wrote T.E., 'and men lounging about. One of these, a Syrian officer, began to question us about our villages... We shook him off at last, and turned away. Someone called out in Turkish... We walked on deafly; but a sergeant came after, and took me roughly by the arm, saying: "The Bey wants you." '

After the failure at Yarmuk, T.E. narrowly avoided capture when a mine failed to detonate under a Turkish troop train. He sat fifty yards away, the exploder by his side, and tried to look like an ordinary Arab while the train rolled past. The drawing is by Kennington.

Deraa station, on its opening day, 1 September 1908.

This was the start of a terrible ordeal. T.E. was enrolled as a soldier, and then told that he might get leave the next day if he fulfilled the Bey's pleasure that evening. He was then taken to the Bey – who was probably not the Governor of Deraa, but the garrison commander, Bimbashi Ismail Bey, or the militia commander, Ali Riza Bey. The Bey began making homosexual advances to Lawrence, fawning on him, pawing him, and kissing him. At last, angered by T.E.'s lack of co-operation, he sent him out to be punished. Four men held him down while he was whipped and kicked, until there was 'a roaring, and my eyes went black: while within me the core of life seemed to heave slowly up through the rending nerves...' The next thing he knew was that he was being dragged about by two men, each disputing over a leg, while a third rode him astride. Later, he was taken to be washed and bandaged, and left in a room from which he managed to escape in the early morning. An Arab gave him a lift on his camel to the nearest village, where he rejoined Faris.

That night he felt, not for the first time, that he wished to have no more to do with Arabia; but he had always tended to despise physical things, and his will told him that insults done to his body should not be treated seriously. On the way back to Azrak, his spirits were revived by the generosity of a raiding party, who let him and Faris pass unplundered, recognizing that Lawrence and his comrades deserved men's homage. Later, after the war and the Peace Conference, his experiences in Deraa preyed more horribly on his mind; and then he wrote that it was on that night in Deraa that the citadel of his integrity had been irrevocably lost.

A pen and water-colour sketch by James McBey of the entry of the Allies into Jerusalem in December 1917. Allenby can be seen on foot in the centre.

The news at Azrak was that Abd el Kader had ridden madly into Turkish territory, and announced that he was taking over the area of Jebel Druse in the name of Hussein of Mecca; he also promised to cut off the head of Jemal Pasha, the Turkish Commander-in-chief in Syria. When he was arrested and sent to Damascus, he rapidly swung round to the side of the Turks, and was now acting as an agent provocateur among Syrian nationalists. T.E. decided to return to Akaba, and on 22 November, handing his remaining money over to Ali, he left with his attendant Rahail.

On the following day, at noon, they were waylaid by four bandits who covered them with rifles, and told them to dismount. Lawrence simply laughed at them. The bandits were puzzled; and then Lawrence insulted them. Astonished that anyone should provoke armed men, they suspected a reserve of men somewhere in the offing, and allowed T.E. and Rahail to escape unhurt. They continued to ride hard for Akaba, despite T.E. falling ill with a bad bout of fever: at one time he felt that his personality had split into parts, one of which was mechanically riding, while another hovered above and leaned down, asking what he was doing; and a third talked and wondered. They reached Akaba on the night of the 25th, and T.E. flew immediately to Allenby's H.Q. in Gaza.

When Lawrence found that Allenby was not much worried by the failure at Yarmuk, he was able to relax among fellow-Englishmen, and to enjoy the reputation which his exploits had won for him. Cairo was dominated by the names of Allenby and Lawrence; and feelings that his own reputation was rather overdone sometimes led T.E. into what appeared to be mock modesty. But he defended the Arabs even to Colonel Meinertzhagen, who told him that they were just looters and murderers; and on 11 December he took part in the official entry into Jerusalem, gaily joking to his fellow-officers about his uniform and the official appointment of staff officer to Clayton, both of which had been loaned him for the ceremony.

Allenby and Dawnay now told Lawrence that the Arabs could do a useful job by moving north to capture Tafileh, and putting an end to the lightering of enemy food on the Dead Sea. So T.E. returned to Akaba. Here he found that the Turks had made another major effort to take the offensive, but constant raids near Maan and Medina had forced them to keep drawing men off to strengthen weak sections, and they had returned again to the Maan outposts.

The road through Wadi Itm had now been completed, and T.E. congratulated Beaumont and the others on their hard work. Soon, the armoured cars were driven to Guweira, where, wrote Beaumont, 'we were met by expert horsemen who rode bare-backed, like fury, round and round, firing rifles into the air and yelling "Aurans! Aurans!"'

Lawrence with Hogarth and Dawnay.

A Rolls-Royce tender, with Colonel Joyce in the front seat, loaded with kit for Guweira; photographed by T.E.L.

A few days later Colonel Joyce and Lawrence took out the armoured cars, and, after racing over the mud flats in the Mudow-wara direction, they attacked two or three places along the railway line. Beaumont remembers one bridge which they destroyed crashing with a terrific roar: 'fragments of masonry flew in all directions & a huge piece of metal only missed Lawrence by inches.' He also saw one of the Turkish posters which put a price of £20,000 alive or £10,000 dead on Lawrence. T.E. had already taken the precaution of increasing his personal followers to a troop of ninety. 'The British at Akaba called them cut-throats but', he wrote with black humour, 'they cut throats only to my order.'

Sherif Nasir and Nuri Said began the Arab operation against Tafileh, the knot of villages commanding the south end of the Dead Sea, with a successful attack on the nearby station of Jurf. An Arab force from Petra climbed up the snow-covered hills and captured Shobek; and by 16 January 1918, Nasir and Auda abu Tayi had arrived outside Tafileh, which fell to them with little bloodshed. Auda soon had to be paid off and sent back to the desert, because his tribesmen began to quarrel with the Motalga, their blood enemies, but Zeid and Jaafar Pasha had arrived from Petra to take command; and Lawrence came up from Guweira to join them. Together, they began to prepare the villages to face a Turkish counter-attack.

The attack came sooner than expected. Fakhri Pasha rapidly brought up a force of a thousand men, with two mountain howitzers and twenty-seven machine-guns. On the morning of 25 January he fell on some outlying Arab pickets, and by dusk was close to Tafileh, where the news of his advance brought panic. 'Everyone was screaming with terror,' Lawrence wrote for the *Arab Bulletin*, 'goods were being bundled out of the houses into the streets, which were packed. . . . Mounted Arabs were galloping up and down, firing wildly into the air, and the flashes of the Turkish rifles were outlining the further cliffs of the Tafila gorge.' Jaafar Pasha proposed an immediate retreat to the heights above Tafileh, but T.E. persuaded Zeid to stand and fight.

In the morning, the battle began in a haphazard fashion, with some Motalga horsemen and the villagers driving back a body of about a hundred Turkish cavalry. They then seized a ridge lying across the plain which the Turks had to cross in their advance on Tafileh. Lawrence, studying the battlefield, saw that close to the village there was another ridge, about forty feet above the plain, which would make 'a good reserve line, or line of ultimate defence'. He placed twenty of Zeid's personal Ageyl there; and, seeing that the Turks were moving rapidly to outflank the advance ridge, he went forward himself, and suggested that they fall back to the more secure reserve position. By the middle of the afternoon, the Turks had occupied the advance ridge, and were bringing up their machine-guns. But in the meantime, a force of some four hundred and fifty men had gathered in T.E.'s reserve position. Military manuals of the time advocated making either right or left-flanking attacks on an enemy, followed up by a frontal charge. On the Western Front, the extended trenches made flanking attacks almost impossible, and

'Sheikh Lawrence and his hired assassins' was the title which T.E. gave to this photograph of his bodyguard, which he preserved alongside his own photos of the Arab Revolt.

frontal charges were the grave-yard of a generation. But there were no trenches at Tafileh.

Lawrence sent Rasim with eighty riders and five automatics to roll up the enemy's left wing (an Arab machine-gunner later claimed responsibility for this move: 'Suddenly an idea struck me, and I said to myself...'). Another hundred men took three automatics and outflanked the Turkish right wing. Then, with the enemy hard-pressed, the camel-men and levies charged, led by Mohammed el Ghasib carrying the crimson banner of the Ageyl. Soon the enemy centre was pouring back in disorder. It was a text-book victory, and Lawrence was later offered a decoration on the strength of it. The news of the victory was sent at once to Abdulla el Feir, camped far beneath them in the warmth near the southern shore of the Dead Sea; and three days later he rode through the night with seventy horsemen to the lake port of Kerak and destroyed the Turkish flotilla, thus stopping the Dead Sea traffic as Allenby had requested.

There was snow at Tafileh. Life became cold, and in the over-crowded conditions, squalid. For a while T.E. escaped into the world of the *Morte d'Arthur*; but then, in the first week of February, he set off with four followers to collect the money which would be needed for a spring offensive. He spent three nights in the armoured car tents at Guweira before £30,000 worth of gold arrived from Akaba. On the way back to Tafileh, T.E. spent a night at Shobek. He talked of marriage to some Arabs there, and asked how they could look with pleasure on children, 'The embodied proofs of consummated lust'. He had known since a child that he was illegitimate, and his sensitive nature had taken upon itself some of the guilt which his puritanical mother felt for what she had done. This had led him to view the body and its demands with a contempt which set him apart a little from other men, but which strengthened his will and lent him considerable powers of endurance.

Lawrence's photograph of Zeid with two Austrian mountain guns which were captured from the Turks at Tafileh.

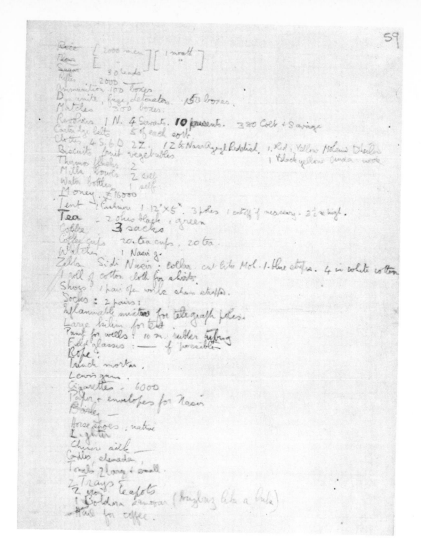

T.E.'s 'shopping list', including everything from 'rice for 2,000 men for one month', to a trench mortar and two iron teapots.

Those powers had already been over-taxed during the Arabian adventure. Now, on the journey from Shobek to Tafileh, his camel broke down in snow drifts, and he had to lead it for miles down slippery snow slopes. Then he handed the money over to Zeid, reconnoitred as far as the edge of the Jordan valley, and returned to find that Zeid had dissipated the entire sum, making payments to local villagers who should only have been paid if wanted on active service. Feeling humiliated and depressed, T.E. rode at once to Beersheba to tell Allenby of the loss. At Allenby's headquarters he found Hogarth, and told him that he had made a mess of things, that he wanted a smaller job elsewhere, and that he could not go on fraudulently posing as the leader of a national movement when he knew how little the promises to the Arabs were worth.

Hogarth said nothing, but took him to breakfast with Clayton. First Clayton and then Allenby emphasized the importance of what the Arabs could do to help the British, by keeping up the fight and drawing off Turkish troops. Allenby promised seven hundred pack camels with personnel and equipment, and £300,000 in gold; and Lawrence, now promoted to the rank of colonel, agreed to carry on. The Arabs were finally to cut the railway between Maan and Medina, capture Maan, and join Allenby in an attack on Damascus.

But in early April, the English failed to take Amman; and Lawrence, waiting at Atara with the Arab force which should have linked up with Allenby's men, retreated southwards towards Maan. Of the two Ageyli boys whom T.E. had accepted into his service in May the previous year, Daud had already died of cold at Azrak; and now, after a skirmish, Farraj was too badly wounded to escape, and T.E. had to shoot him to prevent him being tortured or burnt alive like other Turkish prisoners. Arriving at Maan, he found more bad news. Feisal's troops had captured the high ground overlooking the town, but were not strong enough to capture the town itself. However, T.E. went on to Guweira, and joined Colonel Dawnay in a successful attack on the station at Tell el Shahm. Lawrence took the station bell as a souvenir; and, while the Arabs looted, he joined the armoured cars for further demolition work along the railway. Within three days the eighty miles of line from Maan to Mudowwara, with its seven stations, was wholly in Arab hands. 'All is very well', Lawrence wrote on his return to Cairo, 'and while we have not done all we want, we have done all we could do by ourselves, and it is not at all bad.'

Allenby was now being stripped of troops for the Western Front, and would not attempt another advance before September. In the meantime, there was a real danger that a Turkish counter-attack from Amman would relieve Maan, re-take Aba el Lissan, and

Mudowwara, showing, as T.E. wrote, 'as much of the water-tower as could be got into the field of view of an ordinary camera after Capt. Scott-Higgins had finished with it'.

*Opposite*
An aerial view of Maan.

71

threaten Akaba. T.E. refused to go on to the defensive. Instead, hearing that the Imperial Camel Corps in Sinai was being broken up, he managed to get hold of two thousand riding camels, boldly telling Allenby that he would use them 'to get a thousand men into Deraa any day you please'. T.E. had further strengthened his hand by arranging with Feisal that the regular Arab units still in the south with Abdulla and Ali should be brought up. Allenby agreed to a raid, which would draw off Turkish troops at a vital moment. He told Lawrence that, for his purposes, three men and a boy with pistols in front of Deraa on 16 September would be better than thousands a week before or a week after.

In mid-July news came that Sherif Nasir had been turned out of Wadi Hesa by the Turks, and the danger of an all-out Turkish advance became imminent. Dawnay suggested using Colonel Buxton and the surviving battalion of the Imperial Camel Corps to strengthen the Arab army. Feeling that he now had enough influence to prevent the trouble which a sudden large influx of foreign troops might cause among the Arab tribes, Lawrence agreed, and the battalion was shipped to Akaba. Here T.E. briefed each company on how best to get along with the Arabs. Some of the men were rather disappointed by their first sight of Lawrence, who walked towards them with the effortless sliding gait of a Bedouin, seeming more Arab than English. Indeed, by this time T.E. was living in a sort of mental limbo between the two cultures. On 15 July he wrote to Vyvyan Richards about what appealed to him in the Arab way of life, particularly their 'gospel of bareness in materials', and 'a sort of moral bareness too . . . I think I can understand it enough to look at myself and foreigners from their direction . . . I think abstention, the leaving everything alone and watching the others still going past, is what I would choose today, if they stopped driving one.'

After riding with Colonel Buxton as far as Rumm, Lawrence returned to Akaba, where for the last time he mustered his bodyguard on the windy beach by the edge of the sea, 'the sun on its brilliant waves glinting in rivalry with my flashing and changing men'. Then he rode to Guweira, where he helped Feisal to win over the Shaalan tribe, and passed on an official warning from Allenby: the Arabs should not press ahead too quickly in September, for if the British effort failed, they would be left unsupported. In fact Feisal had already decided to push on to Damascus in any case, and if necessary make a separate peace with the Turks. T.E. was aware of this, but felt that he could not condemn Feisal for it: after all, he might gain more from the Turks than from the British.

Meanwhile, Buxton's Camel Corps had carried out a successful dawn attack on the station of Mudowwara. After meeting the delighted officers and men at Jefer, Lawrence and Joyce drove on to Azrak, to see if there was a route fit for cars. It was not a difficult journey, and they decided that it would make a good working base for the Deraa expedition, with a convenient landing ground for aeroplanes on the mud-flats to the north. Then they returned to Bair, where on 16 August, T.E. passed his thirtieth birthday. He later wrote in *Seven Pillars* that he now took stock of himself: but the relevant chapter, one of painfully morbid introspection, tells us at least as much of T.E.'s state of mind in 1920 and 1921, as of what he was really thinking in 1918. On the surface, at any rate, he was calm and effective, and his leadership had inspirational qualities. One of his drivers remembers him as the principal guest at an assembly of chiefs, 'bare feet tucked under him, swathed as the others, with gold dagger, girdle round his waist, gesticulating from one to the other, forcing his points home one by one'. Beaumont recalls how once, when T.E. was saying goodbye to him and some other men who were on their way to Cairo for a short leave, he told them to come back pure, as though it were a crusade he was leading.

Two days after his birthday, on 18 August, the Camel Corps started northwards, with the object of blowing up bridges and throwing the Turks on the defensive. By the 20th, they had reached Muaggar; but they were spotted by Turkish aeroplanes, and then

Colonel Lawrence in an aeroplane ready for a flight to Azrak.

saw Turkish soldiers in the next village. Instead of attacking and risking heavy losses, the Camel Corps withdrew; but first they sent some Arabs ahead, to tell the villagers that they were an advance party of Feisal's army, which was preparing to attack Amman. As intended, this information reached Turkish ears, and delayed the Turkish push southwards for a week.

T.E. and a detachment of Arabs now led the way towards Azrak, passing by the lone palace of Kharaneh under a brilliant moon, and riding on through multitudes of night-birds which carpeted the earth and wheeled round them in dead silence 'like feathers in a soundless whirl of wind'. They rested at Azrak, and buried tons of gun-cotton in readiness for the Deraa expedition, before returning to Bair. T.E. himself went on to Aba el Lissan, where Joyce and the other English officers told him that their preparations for the expedition were going well.

At this point, the expedition was nearly wrecked by Hussein, who insulted all Feisal's officers by proclaiming that there was no rank higher than captain in the Arab army. Hussein then called Feisal, who refused to accept this ruling, a traitor and an outlaw. Feisal disappeared from public view, and his troops nearly mutinied. T.E. wrote with feeling to the Commandant at Akaba: 'I haven't the least idea if we are at last going to get anywhere

A 'tulip' bomb exploding on the railway line near Deraa.

and do anything or not. My head whirls!' However, by doctoring the exchange of telegrams between Feisal and his father, he got a seemingly repentant message from Hussein. Feisal, who at one point had offered to serve under Lawrence, resumed command; and by 6 September, the final plans had been organized. News came that the Turks had sent a large force into Tafileh; but the Deraa expedition was well under way. By 12 September, Nuri Said, Auda abu Tayi, Tallal el Hareidhin and others were at Azrak with the Arab armies, the Egyptian Camel Corps, and more than three thousand camels. The armoured cars were with them, also two aeroplanes, and a number of English officers including Joyce, Lawrence, Peake, Marshall, Young and Scott-Higgins. The feint at Amman was now completed by sending out gold sovereigns by the thousand to pay for barley belonging to the tribes close to that city, in the knowledge that news of this payment would soon reach Turkish ears. On the 13th, T.E. spent a day alone, far from the army, resting in a lair among the tamarisk, and gathering strength for the coming advance. Then, at dawn on the 14th, the column marched off in the direction of Deraa.

One of their aeroplanes soon shot down an enemy plane which passed overhead, but was itself so badly damaged that their Air Force was reduced to an old BE 12 and its pilot, Junor. But on the next day, Joyce and T.E. blew up a bridge at Umtaiye, cutting the line from Deraa to Amman. By the 16th, the day for which Allenby had asked Lawrence to provide three men and a boy, the main army was over-running the mound of Tell Arar, on the Damascus railway, only four miles north of Deraa.

After sitting down to breakfast, Peake's Egyptians began systematically demolishing six kilometres of track with six hundred 'tulip' charges: these involved placing thirty ounces of gun-cotton beneath the central sleeper of each ten-metre section of the track. If the charge was properly laid, the metal did not snap, but humped itself two feet in the air like a tulip-bud. As T.E. later wrote, with evident satisfaction: 'The lift of it pulled the rails three inches up: the drag of it pulled them six inches together; and, as the chairs gripped the bottom flanges, warped them inward seriously. The triple distortion put them beyond repair.' Before long a reconnaissance plane came out from Deraa and spotted them, and then six more planes came out and began bombing. The Arabs spread out, and Nuri Said, Joyce and Lawrence fought back as best they could with mountain guns and Hotchkiss, but 'we had no cover for a rabbit'. They were wondering how to get their men away from the area safely, when they heard a new drone in the sky, and saw that Junor had arrived in his shaky old BE 12, and was flying alone towards the eight enemy aeroplanes. Weaving in

Lt. Junor and his B.E. 12 biplane.

and out of them with great skill, he drew them off towards the north. This gave the Arab army half an hour in which to split into small, scattered groups, and begin to move westwards towards Mezerib. Then, incredibly, Junor reappeared, 'attended on three sides by enemy machines, spitting bullets. He was twisting and slipping splendidly, firing back . . .' He managed to land the plane; it turned over in the rough, but he scrambled out – unhurt, but for a cut on the chin – and got clear before a Haberstadt came down and scored a direct hit on his BE 12 with a bomb. Junor then borrowed a car and drove down to the railway line to blow another gap in the rails before escaping with the others.

Joyce and Nuri Said stayed at Tell Arar with a covering force, while Lawrence rode with his bodyguard towards Mezerib. They were bombed continually, and one bomb fell so close that T.E. felt a shock which spun his camel round, and knocked him half out of the saddle, with a burning numbness in his right elbow: 'My camel swung to a spatter of machine-gun bullets. I clutched at the pommel, and found my damaged arm there and efficient.

I had judged it blown off ...' Later that day Mezerib was captured, the telegraph which linked the Palestine army with their homeland was cut, and at sunset T.E.'s evening meal was illuminated by the flames of the burning station. At night, they cut the line twice beyond Shehab, and on the 17th moved to Nisib, destroying another bridge – T.E.'s seventy-ninth – before joining Joyce at Umtaiye.

Tallal el Hareidhin's help was most valuable at this time: T.E. later wrote that he helped them day and night, 'our sponsor and backer in every village. But for his energy, courage and honesty, things would have gone hard with us many times.' Lawrence had also re-established contact with Salim Ahmed, or Dahoum, his protégé of Carchemish days, and gained much useful information from him about Turkish troop movements. But at about this time, he visited Dahoum to find him dying of typhoid. Dahoum's death affected T.E. as strongly as the deaths of his own brothers Frank and Will had done, and later added to his general feelings of bitterness about the results of the Arab Revolt.

Umtaiye commanded Deraa's three railways, but was highly vulnerable to Turkish bombing, and so T.E. rode to Azrak and then flew to Allenby's HQ in Palestine to ask for air reinforcement. He heard good news: Allenby's armies, led by his Generals Chaytor, Chauvel and Barrow, had smashed through the Turkish lines. Allenby now planned that Chaytor and his New Zealand troops should attack across the Jordan and rest at Amman; while Chauvel's Australians and Barrow's Indians should go to Kuneitra and Deraa, and then converge on Damascus. T.E. was asked to assist where possible, but not to attempt to capture Damascus on his own; and he was given three Bristol fighters, with a Handley-Page to supply them with spares and petrol.

The Arab army had withdrawn from Umtaiye to Um el Surab, and T.E. joined them here with the Bristol fighters on 22 September. On that first day, two Turkish aeroplanes were shot down; and when T.E. had collected Feisal and Nuri Shaalan from Azrak, they arrived at Um el Surab in time to see the Handley-Page landing. The Arabs were delighted, firing their rifles into the air, and protesting that this was THE aeroplane, of which all the others were just foals.

The Arab strength at Um el Surab was now some 4,000 men; and when, on the 24th, they heard that the Turkish army were retreating from Amman, Lawrence urged them to take the offensive once again. Three days later they entered Sheikh Saad village, while Tallal captured Ezraa, Auda took el Ghazale by storm, and Nuri captured over four hundred Turkish prisoners whom he had found on the Deraa road.

*Opposite*
End of the campaign: Akaba to
Damascus.

British aeroplanes dropped more news: two Turkish columns,
one of 4,000 and one of 2,000 men, were retreating from Deraa
and Mezerib. T.E. and the men with him decided to let the larger
column pass: they were physically exhausted, and only nine
hundred strong. But the nearer two thousand they would meet,
and they moved rapidly in the direction of Tallal al Hareidhin's
village, Tafas, which they had heard the Turks were approaching.
They arrived to find the Turkish column already marching out of
the village, and they attacked it immediately. The Turkish commander of the lancer rearguard in the village at once ordered that
the inhabitants be killed; and when Lawrence and his men came
close to the village, they found heaps of corpses, from one of
which a little girl of three or four staggered away. Her dirty smock
was red with blood from a lance-thrust through the neck, and she
begged them not to hit her, before falling to the ground and dying
as they watched. In the village itself, dead babies lay around. One
pregnant women had been bayoneted between the legs; and a score
of other dead women had been 'set out in accord with an obscene
taste'. One of the Arabs burst into peals of hysterical laughter.
Tallal himself, who in his agony had ridden a little way apart and
drawn his headcloth about his face, now galloped alone at the main
body of the retreating Turkish column. For a while, both sides
stopped shooting. Then, only a few lengths from the enemy, 'he
sat up in his saddle and uttered his war cry, Tallal, Tallal, twice
in a tremendous shout. Instantly their rifles and machine-guns
crashed out, and he and his mare, riddled through and through
with bullets, fell dead among the lance-points. Auda looked very
cold and grim. "God give him mercy; we will take his price."'

The Bedouin fought with uncontrollable fury, and by nightfall
they had destroyed virtually the entire Turkish detachment. When
the main battle was over, T.E. was unable to prevent the massacre
of a batch of prisoners, and when Captain Peake arrived with the
Camel Corps, T.E. ordered him to collect and guard further
Turkish stragglers as they came in.

The Rualla horsemen had ridden on, taking Deraa station 'at a
whirlwind gallop, riding all over the trenches and blotting out the
enemy elements that still tried to hold the place'. Coming into
Deraa in the early hours of the 28th, T.E. found Nasir already
installed in the mayor's house, helped him set up an effective
administration; and then went out again to meet General Barrow,
who was advancing on Deraa, and invited him into the town as the
Arabs' guest. On the following day Feisal drove in, and installed
himself at the station.

Before dawn on 30 September, Lawrence woke Stirling and his
drivers, and they climbed into the 'Blue Mist', their Rolls tender,

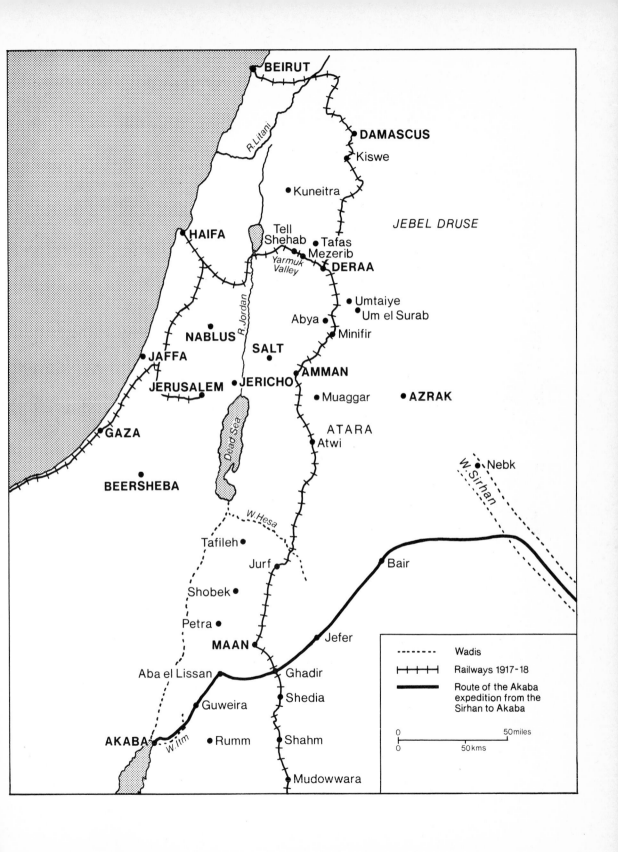

BEIRUT

DAMASCUS

Kiswe

• Kuneitra

*JEBEL DRUSE*

HAIFA

Tell
Shehab
• Tafas
Mezerib
*Yarmuk
Valley*
DERAA

• Umtaiye
• Um el Surab
Abya •
• Minifir

NABLUS

SALT

AMMAN

JAFFA

JERUSALEM  JERICHO

• Muaggar  • AZRAK

GAZA

*ATARA*
Atwi

*W. Sirhan*  • Nebk

BEERSHEBA

*W. Hesa*

Tafileh •

Jurf •

Bair

Shobek •

Petra •

MAAN

Jefer

Aba el Lissan

Ghadir

Shedia

Guweira

*W. Itm*  • Rumm

Shahm

AKABA

Mudowwara

*R. Litani*

*R. Jordan*

*Dead Sea*

| | |
|---|---|
| - - - - - | Wadis |
| +‑+‑+‑+ | Railways 1917‑18 |
| ▬▬▬▬ | Route of the Akaba expedition from the Sirhan to Akaba |

0                    50miles
0            50kms

and set out for Damascus. On the way they passed through the troops of General Barrow, who was advancing at an unnecessarily cautious pace, and came up to the position where Nasir, Nuri Shaalan and Auda were harrying the remnant of the Turkish retreat, a body of about 2,000 men. The Turks eventually fled into the desert, where, that night, Auda and his men killed most of them; until, tired of slaughter, they took the last six hundred prisoner. This completed the destruction of the Turkish Fourth Army.

T.E. had driven on to Kiswe, where he had arranged to meet Nasir. Barrow's army arrived and, wandering among the English soldiers in his Arab uniform, T.E. felt keenly how isolated he had become, even from his own countrymen.

By the early afternoon, the Turks had decided to evacuate Damascus; and, before leaving, they summoned Mohammed Said, leader of the Algerians with whom they had been working, and announced their imminent flight. There had been a committee of Feisal's supporters in Damascus for some months. In the absence of its chairman, Ali Riza, Shukri el Ayubi was holding a special meeting when Mohammed Said and his unpredictable brother Abd el Kader burst in and took control. By sunset, when the last Turkish and German troops were leaving Damascus, the brothers had formed a provisional government.

Not knowing what was happening, Lawrence and Nasir sent Arab horsemen into Damascus to try to make contact with Shukri. By midnight, there were several thousand of these armed men in Damascus, and an Australian cavalry brigade had entered the north-western outskirts of the city.

T. E. Lawrence arriving in Damascus.

At dawn the next morning, the 31st, Nasir and Nuri rode into Damascus and T.E. and Stirling followed them by car. Their driver later recalled the excited scenes as citizens thronged the streets, sang songs, shouted themselves hoarse, while some of the Arabs fired into the air, and a cry from a nearby minaret called them to prayer. Lawrence himself found it 'a nerve-shattering experience', to hear 'a thousand people calling out my name in gratitude'. At the Town Hall, he acted quickly against the Algerian brothers, who he knew would not be reliable supporters of Feisal and his family. When General Chauvel came into the city, he told him that Shukri had been elected as acting-Governor, and advised him to keep his forces outside Damascus for the time being. Then, backed by Nasir, Nuri, and the Rualla horsemen, he actually deposed Mohammed Said and Abd el Kader; and helped with the organization of a new administration, arranging for a police force, sanitation, power, street-lighting, a water supply, a fire brigade, the distribution of food, the re-opening of the railway, a new currency, and forage for Chauvel and his forty thousand horse.

During the night of 1 October, Abd el Kader tried to regain power, and there was some rioting. But there were only five dead and ten wounded, and by noon on the 2nd the city was peaceful again. That afternoon Chauvel marched through the city at the head of a large body of troops, and established himself at the Turkish Governor's house. T.E., meanwhile, was finding doctors for the hundreds of Turkish wounded whom he discovered locked in the Turkish barracks without even a nurse to tend them; and later he helped to dig a mass grave for the dead and the dying.

At lunchtime on the 3rd, Allenby arrived. Finding that an Arab administration was in being, he accepted the status quo, and confirmed the appointment of Ali Riza as Military Governor, under Feisal's command. At two o'clock, Feisal galloped into Damascus at the head of forty or fifty Bedouin, to the cheers of the crowd. Inside the Hotel Victoria, Lawrence acted as interpreter while Allenby told Feisal that Britain and France recognized the belligerent status of the Arab forces, and that he himself would recognize the Arab occupation of territory east of the Jordan, from Maan to Damascus, as a military administration under his own supreme control. When Allenby made it clear that France would be the protecting power in Syria, T.E. denied knowing of this plan, but reconciled Feisal to accepting the situation, at least until the war was over. After Feisal had left the room, T.E. refused to work with a French liaison officer, said that he was due for leave, and that he would like to take it. Allenby agreed, and T.E., who had been in some danger of assassination ever since entering Damascus, left for Cairo.

The headquarters of the Hejaz
army, Damascus, on 6 October
1918.

He had brought the Arabs a long way; as his fellow-officers
realized, the encouragement of the revolt of Sherif Hussein's family
from Turkey, which ended in the capture of Damascus, was something that no one else could have achieved, even with unlimited
gold. At the same time, he had made a vital contribution to the
British success. Allenby later wrote that: 'His co-operation was
marked by the utmost loyalty, and I never had anything but praise
for his work, which, indeed, was invaluable throughout the
campaign.' But now the fighting in the Middle East and in Europe
was virtually over; it would soon be time for negotiations and
settlements, and T.E. wrote from the Grand Continental Hotel,
Cairo: 'I wonder how the Powers will let the Arabs get on ...'

But he did not intend merely to wonder. As we have seen, he
had long known of the Sykes–Picot agreement for carving up the
Middle East and dividing it between France and Britain. Since
early 1918 he had also known of the Balfour Declaration, by
which the Foreign Secretary had announced that the British
Government looked favourably upon the establishment in Palestine
of a national home for the Jews. By agreement with the Zionists,
a British Protectorate would replace the international administration of Palestine envisaged by the Sykes–Picot agreement; though

nothing was to be done which might prejudice 'the civil or religious rights of existing non-Jewish communities in Palestine'.

Lawrence is still blamed by many Arabs for helping to create Israel. It is worth remembering that he had no hand in the Balfour Declaration of 1917; that it would have been difficult for anyone to foresee the vicious anti-Jewish policies in central Europe which led to massive waves of Jewish immigration into Israel, and almost inconceivable that within thirty years a future British Government would have allowed themselves to be thrown out of Palestine by Zionist terrorists. T.E. certainly felt that the Jews would be a beneficial influence, spreading wealth and culture in the Arabian world; but it was always his view that the Jews should never be allowed to become so strong that the Arabs could not 'pull their teeth'.

He knew, then, of the Sykes–Picot agreement and the Balfour Declaration; but he also knew of the Declaration to the Seven – the Seven were a group of leading Syrian nationalists – by which, in June 1918, Britain had promised unlimited Arab sovereignty over land captured by force of Arab arms. By 20 October, with the end of the Great War in sight, he was back in London, telling King George V that he could not accept the insignia of the CB and DSO,

Arrival of King Hussein at Government House, Jeddah, on Independence Day, 1918.

Allenby, Prince Feisal, and Lloyd George at London's Guildhall, 1919.

which he had been awarded during the war, until British promises to the Arabs had been fulfilled. Nine days later, he attended a session of the War Cabinet, and pressed Arab claims upon them. In the report which he was asked to write, he insisted on Feisal being made King of Syria, in defiance of French colonialist ambitions; and on at least a nominal Arab government in Iraq. A few days later he sent a telegram to Feisal, proposing that he should come to the Paris Peace Conference to represent King Hussein.

Feisal's cause had been advancing itself in the Middle East. The Hejaz flag was flown from Government House in Beirut, Syria. After French protests, Allenby's troops removed it. But this brought about the immediate danger of further Arab risings, this time against the Allies. So street criers throughout Arabia were ordered to announce that the people liberated from Turkish rule would be able to set up their own national governments.

Feisal came to France, and then went on to England, where he was received by the Foreign Secretary, Balfour; and also by George V. Then, at a meeting in early December between Feisal, Lawrence and Weizmann (the Zionist leader), Feisal agreed to make room for four or five million Jews in Palestine, who would have a share in the government without encroaching on Arab rights. In return for this, he would get Jewish money and advisers to help him in Syria. When an official document was signed on 3 January, Feisal added a proviso that he would not be bound by it unless the Arabs were given their promised freedom. Five days later T.E. wrote to a friend, telling him that he was off to Paris, and that, at present, everything was evenly balanced.

Despite the worries which had tormented T.E. from time to time, he now saw the chance to redeem his promises to the Arabs, and he worked passionately hard to do this. He gave the impression in Paris of a man at the height of his powers, 'never giving himself away, playing one person against, or with, the other, always towards some end.' J. M. Keynes wrote later that T.E. was at this time fully in control of his nerves, 'quite as normal as most of us in his reactions to the world. He had of course his aloofness, and his mingled like and dislike of publicity, but, reckoned nervously, he was a fit man.' Winston Churchill described how, 'from amid the flowing draperies his noble features, his perfectly chiselled lips and flashing eyes loaded with fire and comprehension shone forth. He looked what he was, one of nature's greatest princes.'

During the first sitting of the Conference, Balfour forgot to ask for delegates to be allotted to the Hejaz; but that night T.E. dined with Balfour while a friend dined with Lloyd George, and on the following day they secured two delegates. President Wilson of the

A portrait of T. E. Lawrence by Augustus John.

United States of America was committed to the ideal of self-determination, and towards the end of January T.E. wrote in his diary that the campaign to win American co-operation in the Middle East was going well. To his parents he wrote that he had seen ten American journalists, 'and given them all interviews, which went a long way. Also President Wilson, and the other people who have influence ...' By the end of March, the Conference had planned a Commission of Enquiry for Syria, to find out from the people what sort of government they wanted. Geoffrey Dawson, the Editor of *The Times*, who shared many of T.E.'s views about the future of the Middle East, now wrote to tell Lawrence that it would be easy to get him elected to a Fellowship of All Souls, from where, once his present job was satisfactorily completed, he could write his account of the desert war. T.E. approved of this idea, and Dawson used his influence to have him elected to All Souls later in the year.

The French, however, sabotaged the Commission by failing to appoint their members; the two British and Americans went to Syria, but the British gave up when it became clear that the French would not co-operate. Hogarth was one of them, and he wrote that he felt 'sick at heart at all this fiasco and the melancholy consummation of four years' work ... I hate the idea of ever setting foot in an Arab land again.'

At the beginning of April, T.E. had some bad news from home: his father had died of pneumonia after catching the Spanish 'flu which was ravaging Europe. Meinertzhagen, talking to Lawrence

T. E. Lawrence with the American publisher F. N. Doubleday; they had met in Paris in early 1919 at a dinner for American journalists. Doubleday later wrote of their meeting: 'My next-door neighbour was a very young-looking man, of, I should say, not more than 27 or 28, who talked with extraordinary brilliancy, and with whom I struck up quite a friendship, as one sometimes does on such occasions, but not very often with an Englishman.'

'A literary method', by Eric Kennington, a comment upon T.E.'s character sketches in *Seven Pillars*. George Bernard Shaw wrote: 'I had to cut out and rewrite several passages that were extremely libellous. He shewed these passages, with my revisions, to the victims, and expected them to be amused.'

in Paris, found him thoroughly depressed, and beginning to feel that if he wrote the truth about the British role in Arabia, he would be entirely discredited. At last Feisal's case was officially heard in Paris. He recited a chapter of the Koran verse by verse while T.E., apparently acting as interpreter, made the necessary speech. It was not enough. A decision was postponed pending the report of the two American members of the Commission to Syria, who had decided to carry on in spite of the French. Feisal returned to Syria to wait upon events.

Lawrence decided to travel to Cairo to collect the papers which he needed for his proposed history. The aeroplane in which he travelled crashed at Centocelle in Italy. The pilot was killed, and T.E. had broken ribs, a broken collar-bone, and severe concussion. He later wrote vividly: 'when a plane shoots downward out of control, its crew cramp themselves fearfully into their seats, for minutes like years, expecting to crash: but the smoothness of that long dive continues to their grave. Only for survivors is there an after-pain.' When he did arrive in Egypt, it was to find that the French and even his own Foreign Office suspected him of having gone out in order to stir up trouble in Syria.

Returning to Paris, he worked frantically hard, writing as much as 30,000 words in 24 hours. His book was to be called *Seven Pillars of Wisdom*, the title of the travel book which he had written at Carchemish before the war, but destroyed in MS. In further affectionate memory of those happy days, he dedicated it to 'S.A.' – probably in memory of Salim Ahmed, though the 'A' may have been Arabia; and, to tease future biographers, he dropped all sorts of contrary hints which have led to whole chapters of idle speculation.

As he wrote, he compared his hopes with his achievements at Paris, and this led to times of deep depression, when things with which he had once coped began to take on a new significance. He told Meinertzhagen not only that he had been involved in a huge lie, but about how he was fighting between the limelight and utter darkness; how his father and mother were never married; how he had been degraded at the hands of the Turks in Deraa.

More hopeful news arrived when the American Commission reported that a French mandate would be wholly unacceptable in Syria, as would a Jewish state in Palestine, or a prolonged rule by the British in Iraq.

T.E. had finished his first draft of *Seven Pillars* by the end of August, and he now revived his undergraduate plan of setting up a printing press with Vyvyan Richards. He bought a field at Pole Hill, Chingford, and wrote to Richards that he felt 'years more settled in mind'. Soon after this, he wrote to *The Times*, urging that weight and expression should be given to the opinions of the Arabs.

Britain and France, however, had once more been discussing a Middle East carve-up; and on 13 September 1919 Lloyd George and Clemenceau agreed that British troops would soon withdraw from Cilicia, Syria and the Lebanon, in preparation for a French take-over in the whole of Syria; while Britain was to have mandates in Palestine, Iraq, and Transjordan. Feisal came to London and made bitter protests; and Lawrence, brought in to persuade Feisal to accept the agreement, told Lord Curzon that he would do nothing unless Feisal received pledges about the Arab character of local government in Mesopotamia. He pointed out that 'French in Syria as Britain in Mesopotamia' would not help the French much if Mesopotamia was given Dominion status; and he urged that Feisal should be allowed to keep Damascus and Deraa.

A plan by Professor William Yale of the American Commission in Paris brought T.E. fresh hope in October, as it would give most Arab states a large measure of self-government. Two Arab states would be set up in Mesopotamia under British protection, and an Arab state ruled by Feisal would be confirmed in Syria, under French protection. Britain would have a mandate over Palestine, where Zionists would be allowed to settle, while France would have a mandate over the Lebanon.

For a while it seemed that the British cabinet would accept Yale's plan, and T.E. at once drafted a letter to Lloyd George, telling of his relief at getting out of the affair 'with clean hands'. But the plan fell through. Feisal made a separate peace with

Clemenceau, which allowed him to keep Damascus and the interior; and in the following April the Allies officially gave the mandate for Syria to France.

In London the popularization of T.E. as 'Lawrence of Arabia' had begun, with a series of illustrated lectures by the American journalist Lowell Thomas. They were so successful that they filled the Albert Hall. T.E. went to them at least five times, un-announced, enjoying the glamour and honour, but preferring to remain on the side-lines. He had a complex attitude towards his new fame. He was pleased, a natural human reaction. He was also amused, refusing to tell Lowell Thomas whether the anecdotes which sprang up about him were true or not, and entertained by the creation of a legend. In December 1919, he wrote as the PPPPS of a letter to Lionel Curtis, an Oxford friend, about an offer of $12,000 to exhibit himself in character at dances in America. He said that he had refused the offer, but while the glamour of it lasted, had bought himself a very expensive book: 'Result a fear-ful financial crisis, and appeal to myself for economy all round!' But, increasingly, his fame repelled him, as he felt that it was founded upon a false idea of his success. In February 1920 he told Colonel

Nesib and T.E.L., photographed by Lowell Thomas.

All Souls College, Oxford, where T.E. worked on *Seven Pillars*, of which Churchill wrote: 'All is intense, individual, sentient – and yet cast in conditions which seem to forbid human existence. Through all, one mind, one soul, one will-power. An epic, a prodigy, a tale of torment, and in the heart of it – a Man.'

Newcombe that in the history of the world (cheap edition), he was a sublimated Aladdin; but in the eyes of those who knew, 'I failed badly in attempting a piece of work which a little more resolution would have pushed through, or left untouched.' The following year he wrote to a lecturer: 'The more that is said, the less peaceful life for me is, and as I don't want to make money out of the myth about myself, the fun is one-sided.'

Lawrence was now at All Souls College, Oxford, where Robert Graves met him at a guest-night early in 1920. T.E. had a great admiration for writers, and Graves was later able to give him introductions to Sassoon, Blunden and Hardy. Graves became a friend of T.E., who later helped him when he was in financial trouble. He visited T.E.'s rooms in All Souls which contained, among other things, some fine books, three Arabian prayer rugs, the station bell from Tell el Shahm, and a clay soldier from a child's grave at Carchemish. Another of T.E.'s guests commented that the older Fellows appreciated his lively company: they must certainly have had a surprise when one morning they woke to find the red flag of the Hejaz fluttering from a pinnacle!

The situation in the Middle East grew steadily worse. There was an Arab revolt against the government which the British had established in Iraq. Colonel Lawrence wrote more letters to the papers suggesting that if Iraq was made a 'Brown Dominion' and allowed England to buy her oil, there would be a rapid end to the waste of lives and money, which was running at the rate of ten million pounds, or the whole cost of the original Arab Revolt, every four months. He also discussed with Sir Hugh Trenchard, the Chief of Air Staff, Winston Churchill's plan for controlling Iraq from the air, an idea of which Lawrence approved. But nothing was done, and soon there was more bad news, this time from Syria. In April 1920, details of the deal between France and Britain were published, and this led to raids by the Arabs upon French establishments. In reprisal, the French marched on Damascus. By the end of July, they had expelled Feisal.

T.E. was deeply depressed, blaming himself for what had happened; and during this period he often spent the whole morning sitting without moving or talking in his mother's house in Polstead Road. Everything for which he had fought seemed to lie in ruins. Moreover, at the end of 1919 he had lost most of the first draft of *Seven Pillars* while changing trains at Reading station. He had advertised, offering a reward for the return of his manuscript, but there were no replies; and during 1920 he had been writing and correcting a new version, thus plunging himself deeper and deeper into a state of melancholy introspection. He felt that he had failed, and that fate had no more good in store for him. Checking over the rough diary which he had kept during the war, he remembered a poem by W. E. Henley, and made a new entry: 'In Damascus when prayer silence came I knew I was worn tool lying in darkness under bench, rejected for ever by the master.' In his new version of *Seven Pillars*, he wrote that all personal ambition had died in him before he entered Damascus in triumph. But Churchill, who knew him well, wrote later that it was the ordeal of watching the helplessness of his Arab friends which altered him. 'His highly wrought nature had been subjected to the most extraordinary strains during the war, but then his spirit had sustained it. Now it was the spirit that was injured.'

At last, T.E.'s views on Iraq met with some support. Sir Percy Cox was entrusted with forming a provisional Arab government, and the Middle East was put in the hands of Winston Churchill at the Colonial Office. Churchill wanted Lawrence's help, and argued with irresistible force that he could not justify his bitterness about the treatment which the Arabs had received if he left any stone unturned in his efforts to improve their position. T.E. therefore joined Churchill's Middle East Department as an official adviser.

A group at the Cairo Conference, including Gertrude Bell (2nd from left, second row); T. E. Lawrence (4th from right, same row); and Churchill, centre front row, who has Sir Herbert Samuel on his right.

Feisal came to London in December 1920, and Lawrence helped to persuade him unofficially to accept the kingdom of Iraq. In March the following year, there was an official conference at Cairo. The main decisions had already been taken, but there was much persuasion to be done, and soon after the Conference opened, Hussein's third son, Abdulla, complicated the issue by suddenly and unexpectedly marching into Amman and announcing that he would liberate Syria and restore Feisal. Churchill and Lawrence decided that they should allow Abdulla to set up an Arab government in Transjordan, if he would agree to a general settlement, and T.E. was driven to Salt to meet Abdulla and have private talks with him. He spent eight days in Amman, living with Abdulla in his camp, and he found it rather like the life in wartime, 'with hundreds of Bedouin coming and going, & a general atmosphere of newness in the air'. It was a successful mission, and Abdulla accepted the Churchill–Lawrence proposals at a formal meeting in Jerusalem. T.E. and Gertrude Bell now helped to devise a procedure for having Feisal made King of Iraq, and later in the year Feisal was duly elected by 98.6 per cent of the vote, the only other claimant, a minor brigand, having been whisked away to Ceylon.

The job was not yet finished: in July 1921, Lawrence was sent out from Britain with full plenipotentiary powers under the Great Seal of England to negotiate with Hussein, who was refusing to agree to the Cairo settlement. T.E. had made no headway with Hussein when he was transferred to Jordan, where a crisis had developed after French protests that the country was being used as a base for guerrilla attacks. The French had demanded the surrender of some Arab nationalists, and Abdulla was ready to resign his new kingdom. But T.E. strengthened Abdulla's will to stay on, and to refuse French demands. Churchill was delighted with Lawrence, who used his powers vigorously, removing officers, using force where necessary, and eventually restoring complete tranquillity.

There were now secure Arab governments in Transjordan and Iraq, and Hussein ruled in Mecca. T.E., who had done all that any man could have done to redeem British promises to the Arabs, felt that it would not be many years before Arab nationalism turned the French out of Syria. But the settlement had not followed quickly enough upon the triumph of the war, and his experience of power-politics made T.E. unwilling to stay on at the Middle East Department. Churchill refused to accept his resignation for some months, but eventually let him go; and in his final letter of resignation, written on 4 July 1922, T.E. wrote: 'I need hardly say that I'm always at his disposal if ever there is a crisis, or any

The meeting between T.E. and Emir Abdullah at Salt in 1921.

Mrs Sarah Lawrence and her eldest son, Dr Bob Lawrence. At the time of T.E.'s death, they were steaming down the Yangtse river in China, having been involved for some time in missionary work. Sarah was a powerful, dominating woman in many respects; but throughout her life she was plagued by the fear that, because of her sin in living with another woman's husband, not even her family could love her. T.E. found her demands for love embarrassing: 'If you only knew', he once wrote to her, 'that if one thinks deeply about anything one would rather die than say anything about it.' Even on her death-bed she was thinking of her guilt, her favourite saying being: 'God hates the sin and loves the sinner.'

job, small or big, for which he can convince me that I am necessary.'

Using as his base the attic of a friend's office in Barton Street, London, he was now working again on *Seven Pillars*. He slept during the day and worked at night, eating at railway stations and occasionally spending a night in a hotel when he wanted his washing done. He enjoyed none of the peace and rest which he needed to recover from the strain of the last four years, and he felt that even his recent diplomatic successes were overshadowed by his 'fraudulent' role in the Arabian campaign.

Judging himself to be a fraud, he despised himself, and his contempt for physical things deepened until he felt that eating itself was a shameful experience. Feelings of guilt about his illegitimacy, and of humiliation about his experience at Deraa, assumed still more importance in his mind, and he began to feel that he did not deserve to be happy. He wrote to his mother that his stay in Barton Street was 'altogether too pleasant to be allowed to go on for long'; and he added, neurotically, how impossible it was to be alone except in a crowd; and even there, one touch would discharge 'all the virtue you have stored up'. Dr E. H. R. Altounyan, an old friend from Carchemish days, ran him to earth one day, and found him feeling no longer in control of his life.

One has only to read *Seven Pillars* to find the key to what he did next. In it, he talks of having lost ambition for temporal dignities because of the falsity of his position. He writes admiringly of the Ageyl, who took pleasure in subordination, 'in degrading the body: so as to throw into greater relief their freedom in equality of mind'. The Ageyl held servitude to be richer in experience than authority; and, giving their lives to an ideal which they held in common, they transcended the merely personal. Lawrence writes also of the certainty in degradation, of there being an animal level below which one could not fall, adding: 'only weakness delayed me from mind-suicide, some slow task to choke at length this furnace in my brain.' Service and subjection, he thought, could be 'a cold storage for character and Will, leading painlessly to the oblivion of activity.'

So he asked Trenchard to allow him to join the RAF as an ordinary aircraft hand, telling him that writing *Seven Pillars* had put ink fever into him, and that he now wanted to write a book about the Air Force. The book was a genuine plan: he saw a great future for the Air Force, and was also emotionally attached to it after his brother Will's death in the service of the Royal Flying Corps. It has often been suggested that T.E. regarded the RAF as a sort of secular monastery. He himself wrote in 1923: 'do you think there have been many lay monks of my persuasion?' and he certainly had the ascetic leanings of a monk. But the dominant motive behind his joining the RAF was almost certainly the one which he recorded later, in the words: 'I think I had a mental breakdown.'

He was not in good physical shape either, and when he signed up, under the name John Hume Ross, a special chit had to be sent by Sir Oliver Swan, the Air Vice-Marshal, to get him through the medical. He was despatched to the training depot at Uxbridge, where, on the first evening, he shrank from the crowds of men, 'all seeming friends', on the camp paths. He returned to his hut, and lay alone on his bed, a frightened man, wondering how this experiment would end, and whether he could 'end his civil war and live the open life, patent for everyone to read?' Later, other men entered the hut and began a rough-house. T.E. found them tough, crude, but good-humoured.

The first weeks were taken up with fatigues and physical training. 'Fatigues, fatigues, fatigues. They break our spirit upon this drudgery.' Utterly pointless tasks were given to the recruits to keep them busy. Rust was painted over, because no wire brushes were available; sacks in which frozen carcasses had arrived at the butcher's shop were carefully boiled and cleaned, only to be thrown away. And the drill was unnecessarily punishing. Jock Chambers, an RAF friend of T.E.'s, explained its severity by saying that the previous batch of recruits, of whom he had been one, had regarded the drill adjutant, 'Stiffy', as a pretend soldier, and pitched into him. 'There was an awful row, T.E. came into Uxbridge on the back wash.'

There was curious contrasts for 'Ross': once, he was making notes about his life at Uxbridge, when out of his notebook fell his parchment Patent as Minister Plenipotentiary: ' "George" you know "to his Trusty and Well-beloved" . . . "What's that?" asked Peters, the inquisitive. "My birth-certificate", I said glibly, shovelling it out of sight.' On another occasion, fishing out a letter from the pocket of his overalls, which were stiffened and stinking of swill after a day on the 'shit-cart', he found a request for him to become editor of a high-brow literary magazine, *Belles-Lettres*.

The life was hard, and was not made easier by the fact that his aeroplane crash in Italy had caused injuries which made his breathing laboured and painful after much exercise. But he began to feel something inwardly soothing and healing in his new sense of kinship with other Air Force men. At a church parade, when the padre read a lesson about the clash between the flesh and the spirit, he felt, gladly, that he was among men 'too healthy to catch this diseased Greek antithesis of flesh and spirit. Unquestioned life is a harmony.' And, after the last fatigue, riding home with his comrades in the back of a lorry, he found himself 'shrunk into a ball and squatted, hands over face, crying babily . . . I was trying to think, if I was happy, why I was happy, and what was this overwhelming sense upon me of having got home at last, after an interminable journey.'

After six weeks at Depot, 'Ross' was posted to the RAF school of photography at Farnborough. The men in his hut gave him a farewell feast, and he noted that he would never be afraid of men again, having learned solidarity with them. He wrote to the Air Vice-Marshal that he was 'curiously bitten with the chance which you have here of making a first-class show, and am now working mainly to help it on.'

Edward Garnett, the literary critic who became a friend of Lawrence and later edited his letters, was now working on an abridgement of *Seven Pillars*, while the artist Eric Kennington was portraying its main characters. T.E. was also corresponding with George Bernard Shaw and his wife Charlotte. He had met the Shaws a few months before he enlisted, and had recently sent them a MS. of *Seven Pillars* for criticism. G.B.S. had put it on one side, but Charlotte read it, and was full of admiration.

At Farnborough, 'Aircraftman Ross' had hardly managed to get himself transferred to a suitably advanced course, when the press

Bernard Shaw and his summerhouse at Ayot St Lawrence.

Charlotte Shaw, photographed by her husband.

discovered his true identity. The story broke at the end of December that 'Lawrence of Arabia' was serving in the RAF as an ordinary hand. Within weeks, having refused the commission which Trenchard offered him, T.E. had been thrown out of the RAF as an embarrassment. He searched for another haven, and with the help of the Adjutant-General to the Forces, whom he had met in Palestine, he was able to enlist in the Tank Corps on 12 March 1923, under the name of T. E. Shaw.

Soon he was established in Hut 12, 'B' Company, at Bovington Camp near Wool in Dorset. But the combined shocks of being dismissed from the RAF, and of finding conditions in the Tank Corps almost intolerable, undermined the fragile structure of happiness and self-confidence which he had shored up on the ruins of his breakdown. Here the men seemed to have no ambition, no hope. He was kept awake night after night listening to 'streams of fresh matter from twenty lecherous mouths'; and his gloomy introspection and hatred of physical things returned, and become more obsessive than ever. To Lionel Curtis he wrote that the world would be a better place without human beings: 'We are all guilty alike, you know... isn't it true that the fault of birth rests somewhat on the child?'; that the only rational conclusion to human argument was pessimism; that he would not even jump in the sports as it was a physical activity; that his mind galloped down twenty divergent roads at

Yours

The Army is muck, stink,
& a desolate abomination

T.E. on a motorbike, talking to
its manufacturer George Brough.

once; that his only relief was to go for a ride on his Brough
motor-bike, and hurl it at top speeds along the road for hour after
hour. 'This sort of thing must be madness, and sometimes I wonder
how far mad I am, and if a mad-house would not be my next (and
merciful) stage . . . yet I want to stay here till it no longer hurts me.'

In this condition of extreme mental distress, it is probable that
T.E. invented the myth of an uncle who made terrible demands
upon him, and enlisted the help of another Tank Corps recruit, John
Bruce, in making sure that the demands, which included tests of
physical endurance, and even birching, were carried out. The
medieval saints, whose lives T.E. had read, had flogged their bodies
to keep them in subjection; and if in his adoption of their methods
there was an element of masochism, harking back to his Deraa
experience, it is difficult to feel anything but compassion for him.

In the camp, his motor-cycle earned him the respectful nickname
of 'Broughie Shaw'. Alec Dixon, a friend of his at Bovington, wrote
later that T.E. had far more influence over the men of his squad

The main room in Clouds Hill. E. M. Forster, who visited Lawrence here, wrote: 'The real framework, the place which his spirit will never cease to haunt, is Clouds Hill.'

*Opposite*
T. E. Shaw in exile in India.

than the sergeant who commanded them. During the summer Dixon sometimes joined T.E. on motor-bike rides, especially to Salisbury, where T.E. loved to wander round the peaceful close; or to Stonehenge, where he would go to watch the sun set behind the ancient standing stones.

After his recruit training, 'Shaw', who was now clerk and storeman in the quartermaster's stores, found an escape from Army life by renting a nearby cottage known as Clouds Hill. It was in a ruined state, but T.E. repaired it with the help of Pioneer-Sergeant Knowles, and nearly every evening he would go there, sometimes with a few friends, to listen to gramophone records of music by Mozart and Beethoven, and to eat picnic meals of stuffed olives, salted almonds and baked beans. Occasionally, he managed a trip to London; and he often went to see Thomas Hardy, who lived with his wife in Dorchester.

But T.E. loathed the Army, and his constant wish was to return to the RAF. In September 1923 he told Lionel Curtis that his thoughts at Bovington centred on the peace of death, and a year later he wrote to Charlotte Shaw, saying that it was silly to fear death more than one feared a dentist from whom one sought relief. 'If only', he added, 'we had some certainty of relief after death.' By June 1925, after one of his many applications to rejoin the RAF had come to nothing, he wrote to Edward Garnett announcing in so many words that he meant to commit suicide once he had tidied up his affairs. George Bernard Shaw and another friend, John Buchan, appealed to the Prime Minister, Stanley Baldwin. Baldwin intervened, and T.E. was transferred to the Cadet College at Cranwell.

The effect on T.E. was tremendous. He wrote to Lionel Curtis that he had everything he wanted from life, and that it made for peace and calm. 'They say the centre of a cyclone is like that. If so, I have pierced through the stormy edges into the heart of things, and there I have suddenly flopped down, feeling very tired and old, now the fighting is all over.' His job was simply to help look after the aeroplanes which the cadets flew; but in his relationships with officers and men he found the give-and-take of a happy family; and he had been given back a sense of purpose: 'Just as the roomy, sordid, clanging momentous hangar is our cathedral, so our day's work in it is worship.' His mind grew healthy, and his attitude to physical things altered for the better: 'Airmen exult to fling their meat about', he wrote, 'each man . . . caring to the utmost for his health and muscularity.' Later, he wrote movingly about the way of life he had grown to love: 'Airmen have no possessions, few ties, little daily care. . . . In the summer we are easily the sun's. In winter we struggle undefended along the roadway, and the rain and wind chivvy us, till soon we are wind and rain. . . . Everywhere a relationship, no loneliness any more.'

He was working again on *Seven Pillars*, preparing, with the help of the Shaws, a subscribers' edition. This was to be a fine, expensive book; and to pay for its production it would also be necessary to bring out a shortened version, *Revolt in the Desert*. Lowell Thomas had also written a book, *With Lawrence in Arabia*: and, to avoid the publicity which the appearance of all three books would inevitably bring, Lawrence applied for a posting abroad, and sailed for India in December 1926.

He worked in the RAF Depot at Karachi, in the Engine Repair Section, where all the aeroplane engines in India came for their periodic overhauls. 'All I do is walk about and do a perambulating clerkly job. . . . The camp is comfortable . . .' he wrote; 'the surroundings are unmitigated desert.' He was soon homesick for England, and wrote to Dick Knowles that in the evening he often went out to the music of the camel bells, sat down under a cactus branch, and wept, remembering Cranwell and the Great North

T.E. at Miranshah. 'The quietness of the place is uncanny.'

Road along which he used to roar on his motor-bike. His exile was cheered by news of the enthusiastic reception given to his books. 'Revolt is selling like apples. Something over 40,000 copies in the first three weeks, they say! That pays off my debts, just about. A service fund gets the surplus, if any!'

In August 1927, he made his new name of T. E. Shaw official by deed poll; and he continued to correspond with Charlotte Shaw, writing to her as openly as he did to Lionel Curtis. She told him about her 'perfectly hellish childhood', with a good gentle father and a dominating mother; and he wrote about his own mother being dominating, and living through her children. He was now working on the notes he had made at Uxbridge and Cranwell, and by March 1928 he had revised them into a book, *The Mint*, which he posted to Edward Garnett, wanting it to be published by Jonathan Cape. But Trenchard, who was allowed to read it, felt that it might be damaging to the RAF: it was truthful about the harshness and stupidity of life at Depot, and reproduced faithfully the coarse language and behaviour of the ordinary airmen. The first public edition was not printed until 1955, and even then the text was considered too shocking to be printed in full.

In May 1928, at his own request, T.E. was transferred to Miranshah, the smallest and most remote RAF station in India, only ten miles from Afghanistan. 'We are only 26, all told', he wrote, 'with five officers, and we sit with 700 India Scouts . . . in a brick and earth fort behind barbed wire complete with search-lights and machine-guns. Round us, a few miles off, in a ring are low, bare, porcelain coloured hills, with chipped edges and a broken bottle sky-line . . . The quietness of the place is uncanny – ominous, I was nearly saying: for the Scouts and ourselves live in different compartments . . . and never meet; . . . we are not allowed beyond the barbed wire by day, or outside the fort walls by night . . .'. He worked as clerk and typist, and in his spare time he was translating the *Odyssey*. He had been offered £800 for this, and had jumped at the chance of earning some money which he felt that he could honourably keep.

Even in this remote place, his past caught up with him. At the end of 1928 there was a rebellion in Afghanistan, and journalists fabricated the story that Lawrence of Arabia and the Government of India were behind it. T.E.'s presence became an embarrassment, and he was rushed back to England by plane and boat so quickly that he had to leave most of his possessions behind. Official attempts to hush up his return fuelled suspicions, and the press hounded him. From Barton Street he wrote to E. M. Forster: 'I am being hunted, and do not like it . . . I have a terrible fear of getting the sack from the RAF.' He also mentioned that some anonymous persons (who were in fact the Shaws) had sent him 'a very large and new and apolaustic Brough: so if my life is saved out of the hands of the hunters, it will be a merry one.' As it was, T.E. talked personally to senior newspapermen about the way reporters were treating him, and he persuaded the politician Ernest Thurtle not to ask questions in the House. The fuss died down, and T.E. escaped with a warning from Trenchard to keep away from newspapers and politicians. He was then given a month's leave, and a posting to Wing-Commander Sydney Smith's flying-boat squadron at Cattewater, near Plymouth.

T.E., or Tes as he became known by Sydney Smith and his wife Clare, had already met the Smiths at the time of the Cairo conference in 1921. They had renewed their acquaintance at Cranwell, where he allowed them to read the finished manuscript of *Seven Pillars*; and it was Sydney who had met him at Plymouth on his return from India, and escorted him up to London. At Cattewater – later renamed Mount Batten – the Smiths found him 'tense and strung up'; but his first reaction was to like the place: 'only 100 of us live in it: the other 50 airmen are natives, and live in the town. The huts and sheds fill the whole of a little promontory (like a petrified lizard's bones) which runs out from a green hill into the Sound, facing Plymouth across about a mile of water ... the airmen say it is a happy place.'

Lord Astor, Wing-Commander Sydney Smith, Lady Astor, George Bernard Shaw, Charlotte Shaw (hiding behind her husband in imitation of T.E., whose feet only are visible on the ladder in the background), Maureen Sydney Smith, and Clare Sydney Smith with two dogs. Clare Sydney Smith later wrote: 'Lady Astor brought George Bernard Shaw down.... After lunch we went down to the slipway where the men were working on one of the flying boats – GBS's hat flew off when he was down looking at the engines, and Lady Astor tried to get someone to drop black paint on his head.'

The next three years were indeed happy ones both for Tes and the Smiths. Sydney Smith was an intelligent and friendly CO, and Tes was popular with his fellow airmen. First he was posted to workshops to examine the marine side of the flying-boat station. The motor-boats used for ferrying and rescue work were always giving trouble; he dismantled the engines himself to study them, and all the technical correspondence was turned over to him. In his free time, when he was not busy translating the *Odyssey*, he often went to the Smiths' house, where he talked, listened to music, and became their close friend. He also found time to crew a Moth seaplane, and dreamed of a world flying-boat cruise which would give him an epic subject for another book; and he met and perhaps inspired Amy Johnson, who was then learning to fly.

In the autmn, he became Sydney's personal clerk, and helped him to organize the Schneider Trophy Air Race – an international event – passing notes to him at meetings with suggestions for out-manoeuvring anyone who was being difficult. During this year, he also discussed a number of service reforms with Sydney. In many cases, he initiated real action by writing letters to influential people about the alteration or abolition of a vast range of things, from the compulsory buttoning of greatcoats to the death penalty for cowardice. At the air race itself, he met many celebrities, and attracted publicity which Lord Thomson, the new Labour Minister

Aircraftman Shaw with RAF officers at trials for the Schneider Trophy race in 1929.

for Air, found most unwelcome. Lord Thomson was particularly
annoyed when a photograph of himself and Aircraftman Shaw was
widely published. Tes came close to being thrown out of the RAF
for a second time; and he was refused permission to crew a Moth
civil aircraft on a European trip. It was at about this time that
some socialists burned 'Lawrence of Arabia' in effigy on Tower Hill,
as the 'arch-spy' of imperialism.

The air race over, Tes and the Smiths were jointly given a
Biscayne baby speedboat, which they christened 'The Biscuit'. Tes
got it into good working order, and took Clare Smith for picnics
in it, motoring along the coast and exploring up rivers: 'We tied
up alongside a bank of weeping willows,' wrote Clare, 'landed our
rugs ... and sat down for a morning's lazy time. Tes took up my
copy of *Vogue* and commented on its advertisements so comically
that I had to roar with laughter ...'. He relaxed in the family life
which he enjoyed with the Smiths, even sharing some days of their
leave to go blackberrying and mushrooming with them.

Then, in February 1931, Wing-Commander Tucker, who was
not a qualified pilot of flying boats, used his rank to take command
of one in the air, and nose-dived it into a calm sea. Tes witnessed
the crash, and directed rescue operations: but the slow duty-launch
took too long to reach the wreck and Tucker and eight others
died. Tes later wrote of a sea of molten-visioned aluminium, in
which 'six of us crushed together in the crushed canister of the
hull were bubbling out their lives'. He was determined that the
truth should not be hushed up, and at the inquest, with the help of
an influential friend, Lady Astor, he arranged for the full story
to be made public. This led to an important reform: command in
the air was officially acknowledged to belong to the pilot, irrespec-
tive of rank.

The tragedy had also made Tes passionately committed to the
development of faster launches; and soon after the crash, Sydney
Smith loaned him to Scott Paine's boat-yard in Southampton to
help in testing them. He became absorbed in the work, and remained happy in it despite the departure of the Smiths before the
end of 1931. An old school friend visited him at about this time,
and found him 'his old self, impish, whimsical, flippant and serious
by turns'.

After newspaper reports in September 1932 dramatized his part
in developing the new launches, T.E. was returned for a while to
ordinary duties. But in the following spring, after angrily applying
for his discharge two years before it was due, he was allowed to
continue his work. T.E. was now given a free hand to travel
round the boat-yards, watching over the Ministry's interests, and
giving advice and help in the development of new kinds of boat,

including armoured target launches. This took him to Bridlington in Yorkshire, where during the winter months of 1934–5 he became a close friend of Flight-Lieutenant Reginald Sims and his wife Hilda. Sims found him 'a completely irresistible, compelling power. I could imagine all men following him to the world's end, or beyond it.'

In his spare time, T.E. had finished his *Odyssey* and done other translation work; and he was making plans for the future. He had already told Charlotte Shaw that when he retired to Clouds Hill in 1935 he would write a book to be called *Confessions of Faith*; this was to embody *The Mint* and other notes of his, and to be about the entry of man into 'that reserved element, the air. ... The purpose of my generation, that's really it.' He wrote to Robert Graves in similar vein, adding that progress today was made by

Armoured target launch at the RAF station, Bridlington. T.E. helped in the development of these fast boats.

*Opposite*

A page from a popular account of his life annotated by T.E. for the benefit of the Sims family.

A photograph of Lawrence taken in early 1935.

# CHAPTER XIII

## LAWRENCE OF ARABIA

A FEW years before the war a young undergraduate at Oxford, desirous of securing for a paper he had to write for an examination some first-hand knowledge of the military architecture of the Crusades, persuaded his parents to give him two hundred pounds and set out on a visit to the little-known desert country of Syria.

He was only a boy, but a very adventurous boy who was bitten with the determination to do things "thoroughly," so on his arrival in the Near East he did not follow the usual path of the tourist, but straightway adopted native costume and set off barefoot into the Arabian desert to learn all he could about a land and a people that had fascinated him ever since he was old enough to read.

For two years this young British boy "lost himself" in the wilds of the desert. At the end of that time he returned to take his degree—with one hundred pounds still left of his original capital!

The other hundred pounds that his two years' travels had cost him were later on to be revealed as the finest investment of our generation for the British Empire. That first visit to Arabia resulted in far more important and spectacular things than writing a thesis. It marked the beginning of a dream—the dream of a united Arabia, a country whose people would stand together, shoulder to shoulder, back to back, instead of carrying on interminable petty revolts and rebellions among themselves.

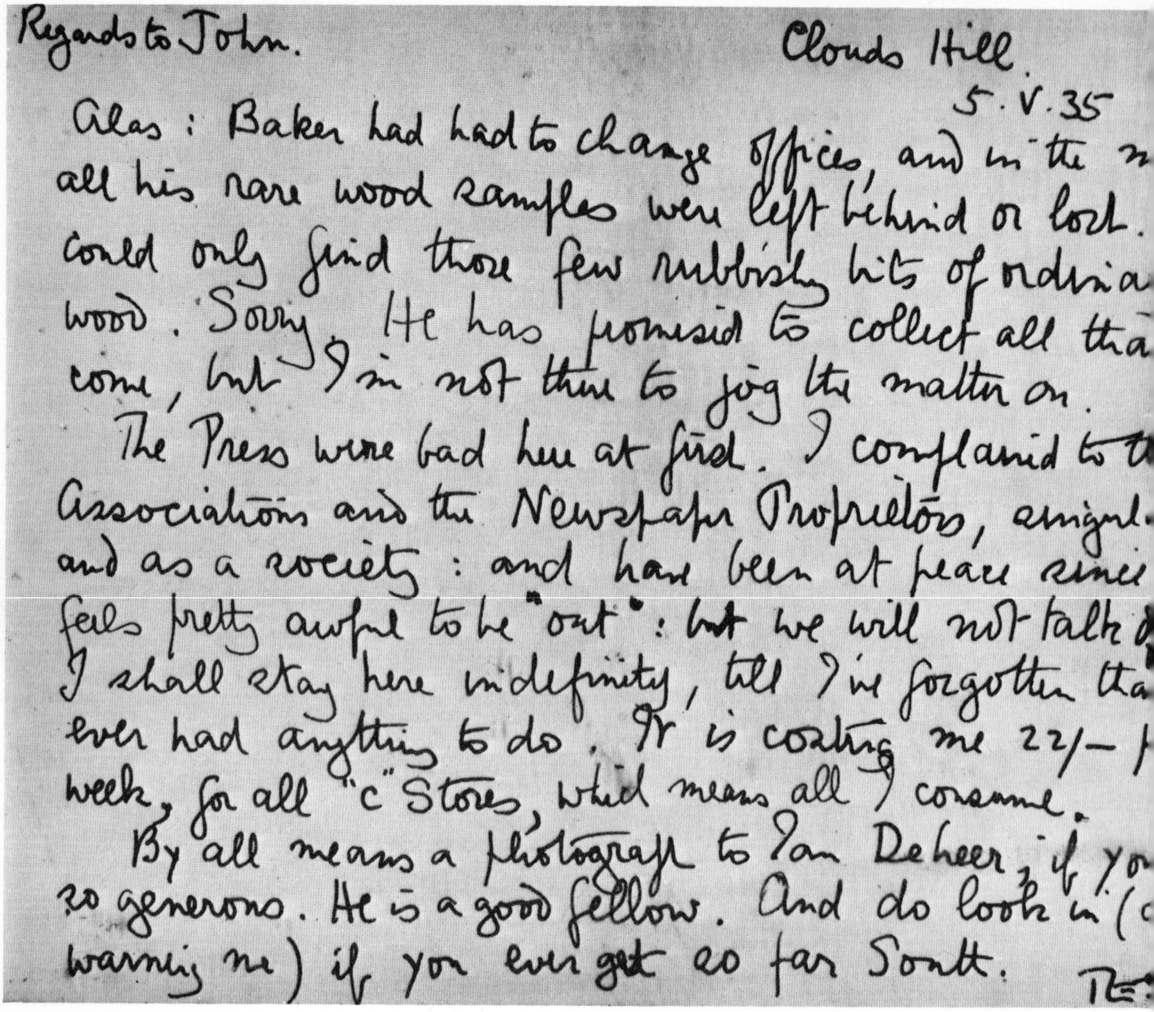

*Regards to John.*

*Clouds Hill.*
*5. V. 35*

Alas: Baker had had to change offices, and in the m
all his rare wood samples were left behind or lost.
could only find those few rubbishy bits of ordina
wood. Sorry. He has promised to collect all tha
come, but I in not there to jog the matter on.

The Press were bad here at first. I complained to t
Associations and the Newspaper Proprietors, singul.
and as a society: and have been at peace since
feels pretty awful to be "out": but we will not talk
I shall stay here indefinitely, till I've forgotten tha
ever had anything to do. It is costing me 22/-
week, for all "c" Stores, which means all I consume.

By all means a photograph to Ian De heer, if you
so generous. He is a good fellow. And do look in (
warning me) if you ever get so far South.

T.E

On leaving the RAF, T.E. had some cards printed with the words 'To tell you that in future I shall write very few letters. T.E.S.' He sent a card to the Sims family, crossing out the printed message, and writing the letter which appears above on the back of it.

the common effort: 'it is the airmen, the mechanics, who are over-coming the air.' He also talked to Pat Knowles about setting up a printing press at Clouds Hill.

In December 1934 he wrote again to Charlotte: 'I wonder how it will be with me … here I am still strong and trenchant-minded, but with nothing in my hand.' But he seemed to be in good spirits, and when he received his leaving gratuity in February 1935 he took a few airmen to see the film *Cleopatra*, which he considered '100%'. On the Saturday before leaving, a young press-man asked his future plans, and he replied in mock anger: 'I shall make a list of all the press representatives in London, and shall then assassinate them one by one. YOUR turn will come in about five years' time.'

Then, on Tuesday 26 February, he took his discharge from the

RAF, 'and started southward by road. My losing the RAF numbed me, so that I haven't much feeling to spare for the while. . . .' The press pestered him, besieging Clouds Hill and damaging the roof. He must have felt tempted to carry out the threat which he had made a few weeks before, but he contented himself with giving one of them a black eye, and complaining to the Newspaper Society. He was then allowed to settle down and adjust to his new way of life.

Early in March it was being rumoured that at some time he might be asked to help reorganize Home Defence, and he told Pat Knowles privately that if this happened, he would feel that he had no alternative but to take the job and delay his printing plans. But it would have needed Churchill or a man like him to entice T.E. back into public life. When Lady Astor wrote, inviting him to one of her famous Cliveden week-ends to meet some politicians, he replied that Clouds Hill was an earthly paradise, and that in his present mood, he 'would not take on any job at all. . . . Am well fed, full of company, and innocent-customed.'

Then, on the morning of 13 May, returning from Bovington camp, he was riding at a good speed over a crest of the narrow

A newspaper cutting from the *Western Morning News and Daily Gazette.*

At the funeral. Philip Graves
wrote: 'I went to T.E.'s funeral –
a lovely country & a very nice
little church, a simple Anglican
service … he was a great man …
God rest him. His brother is a
size bigger but oddly like,
charming and with the same
power of disconcerting reply.
Thus when dear old S. F.
Newcombe was being approached
by a reporter who took him for a
general (S.F. has left the army
and is now in business) and was
wondering how to drop the
enquirer, A.W.L. let go the
words "No, he's an asbestos
merchant", whereat the reporter
left this uninviting prey …'
Churchill *(below)* wrote, more
sadly: 'I had hoped to see him
quit his retirement and take a
commanding part in facing the
dangers which now threaten the
country.'

road, probably with a car coming towards him on the off-side, when he suddenly came up behind two boys on bicycles. Braking sharply, he changed down into second gear, and tried to swerve out of the way. He was too late to avoid colliding with one of the bicycles, though the boy on it was thrown clear and was not seriously hurt. T.E. himself had crashed into the road. He lay there unconscious, his skull fractured and his face covered with blood. Taken to the army hospital at Bovington, his condition grew gradually worse, and he died six days later, on Sunday 19 May, without regaining consciousness. The King himself sent a telegram of condolences to the family.

T.E. was buried in the village cemetery at Moreton, after a funeral service in the church attended by old friends and comrades, including many who had fought with him in the desert. It is a remote, peaceful place; and T.E. lies at rest in the shade of a silver cedar.

Eric Kennington carving the effigy of T. E. Lawrence, which he worked at for four years, and which now rests in Wareham church.

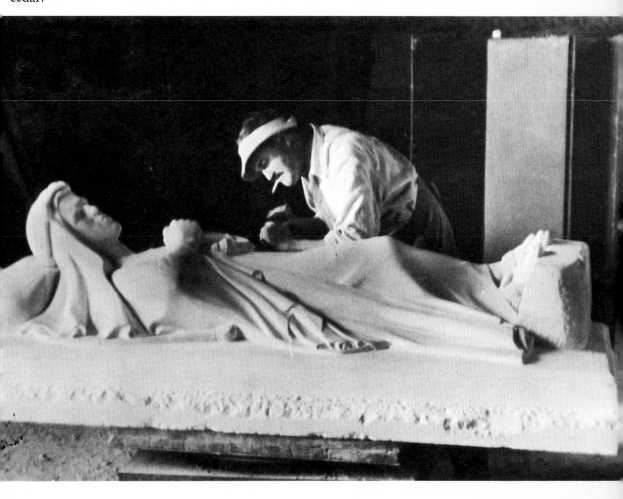

# CHRONOLOGY

1888 16 August: Lawrence born in Tremadoc, North Wales.

1896 Lawrence family settles at 2, Polstead Road, Oxford.

1896–1907: At Oxford High School.

1907 October: to Jesus College, Oxford. Meets Vyvyan Richards.

1909 Summer: walk through Syria.

1910 Gains First in Modern History.

1910–11: at Jebail, Syria; learns Arabic from Farida el Akle.

1911 March: at Carchemish under D. G. Hogarth; April: under R. Campbell Thompson. Summer: walk through northern Mesopotamia.

1912 January: with Flinders Petrie in Egypt. Spring: Carchemish under C. L. Woolley. Christmas: in Oxford.

1913 At Carchemish. July: at Oxford.

1914 January: spying in Sinai: February: Carchemish. June:

England. Autumn: War; after delay, into Geographical Section. December: to Cairo, Egypt.

1915 Frank and Will Lawrence killed.

1915–16 Negotiations lead to Sykes–Picot treaty.

1916 Clayton forms Arab Bureau. March: to Mesopotamia. 9 June: Hussein revolts. October: to Hejaz, meets Feisal. November: appointed liaison officer. December: Turks threaten Yenbo.

1917 January: with Feisal to Wejh. March: to Wadi Ais. April: Auda abu Tayi at Wejh. 9 May: starts for Akaba. 27 May: reaches Howeitat. 5–18 June: reconnaissance. 6 July: capture of Akaba. September: destroys Turkish train. October: to Azrak. November: Yarmuk attack fails; the Balfour Declaration; the Deraa incident. December: attacks on railway.

1918 January: battle of Tafileh. February: Zeid dissipates £30,000. April: attack on Tell el Shahm. June: Declaration to the Seven. July: Camel Corps at Akaba. August: gun-cotton to Azrak. 16 September: Arab army near Deraa. 22 September: after short absence T.E. returns with aeroplanes. 28 September: the Tafas massacre; Deraa entered. 30 September: enters Damascus, ousts Algerians, organizes civil administration. 3 October: Allenby recognizes Arab administration; Feisal enters Damascus; T.E. on leave. 29 October: in England, presses Arab claims on War Cabinet. November: War ends. December: talks with Weizmann and Feisal.

1919 January: to Paris for Peace Conference; meets Churchill. March: Commission of Enquiry for Syria, but French uncooperative. April: father dies. Spring: Feisal decision postponed; on way to Cairo, T.E. in air crash; works on *Seven Pillars*. August: to Oxford; buys field at Pole Hill; Lowell Thomas lectures. September: Clemenceau–Lloyd George agreement. October: Yale plan abandoned. November: elected to All Souls.

1920 July: Feisal expelled from Syria. September: new version of *Seven Pillars* completed. December: in Middle East Department of Colonial Office; Feisal to London.

1921 March: Cairo Conference; Abdulla seizes Transjordan; procedure for making Feisal king of Iraq. July: negotiates with Hussein; restores peace in Jordan.

1922 March: meets the G.B. Shaws. Spring: rewrites *Seven Pillars*.

July: resigns from Colonial Office. August: in RAF as John Hume Ross; to Uxbridge. November: to Farnborough. December: Press reveal his identity.

1923 January: discharged from RAF. March: in Tank Corps, as T.E. Shaw; meets J. Bruce. Summer: rents Clouds Hill, Bovington.

1924 March: asks to rejoin RAF.

1925 Further attempts to rejoin RAF. June: suicide threat. July: to RAF Cranwell.

1926 Prepares *Revolt in the Desert*. December: posted RAF Karachi, India. December-January 1927: subscribers' edition of *Seven Pillars* sold.

1927 March: *Revolt in the Desert* published. August: changes name to T. E. Shaw by deed poll.

1928 March: finishes *The Mint*. May: to Miranshah; works on *Odyssey*.

1929 January: sent home from India. March: to Cattewater (Clare and Sydney Smith). September: helps organize Schneider Trophy race.

1931 February: sees flying boat crash. Works on fast launches.

1932 September: on ordinary duties.

1933 Spring: applies for discharge, allowed back on special work.

1935 February: discharge from RAF; to Clouds Hill. 13 May: crash; 19 May: death.

# SELECT BIBLIOGRAPHY
## AND ACKNOWLEDGMENTS

*I acknowledge the use of material from the following books, which I have divided into two lists:*

BOOKS TO BE READ FOR PLEASURE:

Antonius, George, *The Arab Awakening*. London, Hamish Hamilton, 1938.

Garnett, David (ed.), *The Letters of T. E. Lawrence*. London, Jonathan Cape, 1938.

Lawrence, A. W. (ed.), *T. E. Lawrence By his Friends*. London, Jonathan Cape (abridged ed.), 1954.

Lawrence, M. R. (ed.), *The Home Letters of T. E. Lawrence and his brothers*. Oxford, Blackwell, 1954.

Lawrence, T. E., *The Mint*. London, Jonathan Cape, 1955.

Lawrence, T. E., *Seven Pillars of Wisdom*. London, Jonathan Cape, 1935.

Sims, R. G., *T. E. Lawrence*. Congleton Office Services.

Sydney Smith, Clare, *The Golden Reign*. London, Cassell, 1940.

Wilson, J. M. (ed.), *Minorities* (T. E. Lawrence's collection of poems). New York, Doubleday & Co., 1972.


BOOKS FOR THE SCHOLAR OR LOVER OF CONTROVERSY:

Courtney, W. L. (ed.), *Fortnightly Review* Vols. XCIX *et seq*. London, Chapman & Hall, 1917–18. ('Review of the War' sections interesting on the siege of Kut and for an impression of how the Revolt appeared to people in England at the time.)

Doubleday, F. N., *The strange character of Colonel T. E. Lawrence*. New York, printed privately, 1928.

Graves, Sir Robert, *Storm Centres of the Near East*. London, Hutchinson, 1933.

Graves, Robert, and B. H. Liddell Hart, *T. E. Lawrence to his Biographers*. London, Cassell, 1963.

Knightley, P., and C. Simpson, *The Secret Lives of Lawrence of Arabia*. London, Nelson, 1969. (But, in connection with this, see A. W. Lawrence's letter, published in *The Times* on 22 November 1969, which casts grave doubt on the reliability of John Bruce's narratives, among other things.)

Lawrence, A. W. (ed.), *Oriental Assembly*. London, Williams and Norgate, 1939. (Contains reports for the *Arab Bulletin*, etc.)

Meinertzhagen, Colonel Richard, *Middle East Diary 1917–1956*. London, Cresset Press, 1959.

Mousa, Suleiman, *T. E. Lawrence, an Arab View*. Oxford University Press, 1966. (I have relied particularly upon A. W. Lawrence's postscript, which contains evidence about (*a*) responsibility for the Akaba expedition, and (*b*) what really happened at Tafas.)

Richards, V., *Portrait of T. E. Lawrence*. London, Jonathan Cape, 1936.

Storrs, Sir R., *Orientations*, London, Ivor Nicholson and Watson Ltd., 1937.

I have of course read Aldington and Nutting, but feel that their books give profoundly mistaken views of T.E., and I have not had to make use of them.

I also acknowledge the use of un-published material from documents or copies of documents in:

*The British Museum* T.E.'s wartime diaries, Add. MSS. 45983 and 45915. Correspondence with Charlotte Shaw, Add. MSS. 45922 and 45903.

*The Codrington Library* Correspond-ence with Lionel Curtis.

*Jesus College Library, Oxford* A letter to Lionel Curtis.

# LIST OF ILLUSTRATIONS

photographed at Carchemish. *By courtesy of the Trustees of the British Museum*

20 T. E. Lawrence, Leonard Woolley, and Arab workers at Carchemish. *By courtesy of the Trustees of the British Museum*

23 Street scene in Cairo, *c.* 1915. Photo Radio Times Hulton Picture Library

24 Sherif Hussein of Mecca. *Imperial War Museum, London*

25 General Townshend at Kut, with the staff of the Sixth Division. *Imperial War Museum, London*

26 Street scene in Jeddah; photograph taken by Ronald Storrs, October 1916. *Imperial War Museum, London*

27 'Bringing a 5" Howitzer to Rabegh'; the first photograph taken by T. E. Lawrence in the Hejaz. *Imperial War Museum, London*

29 The Emir Feisal; painting by Augustus John, 1919. *Ashmolean Museum, Oxford*

30 The quay at Yenbo. *Imperial War Museum, London*

31 Garland and Colonel Clayton. *Imperial War Museum, London*

32 Captain T. E. Lawrence in Arab dress. *Imperial War Museum, London*

33 Outside Feisal's tent in Nakhl Mubarak. *Imperial War Museum, London*

Feisal and his army retreating to Yenbo; photo by T. E.

Lawrence. *Imperial War Museum, London*

35 T. E. Lawrence's Turkish opponents and their supporters, including Fakhri-ed-Din Pasha, Ibn Rashid, and Ibn Rashid's standard-bearer. *Imperial War Museum, London*

36–7 Sherif Feisal with Ageyl bodyguard on first stage of journey to Wejh, between Nakhl Mubarak and Yenbo; 3 January 1917. *Imperial War Museum, London*

39 Emir Feisal's army during a review at Wejh, January 1917. *Imperial War Museum, London*

40 Lieutenant-Colonel S. F. Newcombe; March 1917. *Imperial War Museum, London*

Representatives of tribes coming in under a white flag to swear allegiance to Feisal at Akaba. *Imperial War Museum, London*

41 Ali ibn Hussein (left) and his brother Abdulla (centre). *Imperial War Museum, London*

42 Captain Hornby. *Imperial War Museum, London*

43 Auda abu Tayi of the Howeitat; pastel by Eric Kennington. By permission of C. J. Kennington

44 Sherif Nasir (seated, right foreground). *Imperial War Museum, London*

45 Kalaat Sebail at Wejh, 9 May 1917; the party on the day before it started for Sirhan. *Imperial War Museum, London*

46 Farraj and Daud. Photo courtesy of Mr and Mrs T. W. Beaumont

48 Auda abu Tayi (centre) and Sherif Nasir. *Imperial War Museum, London*

49 Letter dated 11.8.20 from T. E. Lawrence to L. M. Gotch, with T.E.'s map of the Akaba campaign. Collection Paul Gotch, Anthea Barker and Christopher Gotch.

52 The triumphal entry of Feisal's forces into Akaba, 6 July 1917. *Imperial War Museum, London*

53 Discussing the terms of the Turkish surrender at Wadi Itm near Resafl; 5 July 1917. *Imperial War Museum, London*

T. E. Lawrence at Akaba. *Imperial War Museum, London*

55 Field-Marshal Viscount Allenby (right) with General Sir Reginald Wingate, British High Commissioner in Egypt. Photo Radio Times Hulton Picture Library

56 Jaafar Pasha, Feisal and Lieutenant-Colonel Joyce in Wadi Kuntilla, August 1917. *Imperial War Museum, London*

57 H.M.S. *Humber* at Akaba, with Chatham pier in the foreground. *Imperial War Museum, London*

Operations on a fuse and interested spectators, at Muwallado. *Imperial War Museum, London*

58 Arab tribesmen looting a Turkish train during a raid on the Hejaz Railway; a still from David Lean's film *Lawrence of Arabia*. Photo National Film Archive

59 T. W. Beaumont after two months' service in the army, on his first weekend pass, January 1916. Photo courtesy of Mr and Mrs T. W. Beaumont

Junction of the Wadi Rumm with the Akaba–Guweira road, looking north. *Imperial War Museum, London*

61 View of the old walls of Azrak. *Imperial War Museum, London*

62 First and biggest girder bridge in the Yarmuk valley. *Imperial War Museum, London*

63 'A Miscarriage'; cartoon by Eric Kennington. By permission of C. J. Kennington

Deraa station on its opening day, 1 September 1908. *Imperial War Museum, London*

64 The Entry of the Allies into Jerusalem; pen and watercolour sketch by James McBey; December 1917. Imperial War Museum, London. Photo Eileen Tweedy

65 Colonel T. E. Lawrence with Commander D. G. Hogarth and Colonel Alan Dawnay. *Imperial War Museum, London*

66 Rolls-Royce tender, with Colonel Joyce in the front seat and Corporal Lowe at the bonnet, loaded with kit for Guweira. *Imperial War Museum, London*

67 T. E. Lawrence with his body-guard. *Imperial War Museum, London*

68 Zeid with Austrian mountain howitzers captured from the Turks at Tafileh. *Imperial War Museum, London*

69 T. E. Lawrence's 'shopping list' of supplies for his men during the Hejaz campaign. British Museum, Additional MS. 45915 (The Lawrence Papers). By permission of Mr A. W. Lawrence and the T. E. Lawrence Trustees

70 Aerial view of Maan. *Dorset County Museum, Dorchester*

71 The remains of the water tower at Mudowwara, after it was blasted by Captain Scott-Higgins. *Imperial War Museum, London*

73 Colonel T. E. Lawrence in airplane ready for a flight to Azrak. Library of Congress, Washington. Photo The Matson Photo Service

74 Tulip bomb exploding on the railway near Deraa. *Imperial War Museum, London*

76 Lieutenant Junor and his B.E. 12 biplane. *Dorset County Museum, Dorchester*

80 T. E. Lawrence arriving in Damascus. Photo courtesy of Rolls-Royce Motors

82 The Headquarters of the Hejaz Army, Damascus; pen and water-colour sketch by James McBey, 6 October 1918. Imperial War Museum, London. Photo Eileen Tweedy

83 Arrival of King Hussein at Government House, Jeddah, on Independence Day, 1918. *Imperial War Museum, London*

Lord Allenby, Lloyd George and Emir Feisal at the Guildhall, London, in 1919. Photo The Press Association Ltd

85 T. E. Lawrence; pencil sketch by Augustus John. *National Portrait Gallery, London*

86 T. E. Lawrence with the American publisher F. N. Doubleday. Photo British Movietone Film Library

87 'A Literary Method'; cartoon by Eric Kennington. By permission of C. J. Kennington

89 Nesib el Bekri and T. E. Lawrence, photographed by Lowell Thomas at Akaba, 1918. Photo Humanities Research Center Library, The University of Texas at Austin

90 All Souls College, Oxford. Photo Edwin Smith

92 Group photo taken at the Cairo Conference, 1921. Photo Radio Times Hulton Picture Library

93 T. E. Lawrence and Emir Abdulla during Lawrence's visit to the Middle East in 1921. Library of Congress, Washington. Photo The Matson Photo Service

94 Mrs Sarah Lawrence and her eldest son Dr Robert Law-

rence; photograph taken when Mrs Lawrence was 95 years old. Photo Humanities Research Center Library, The University of Texas at Austin

97　A snapshot of Charlotte Shaw taken by George Bernard Shaw. Photo courtesy of Harold White

George Bernard Shaw in his summer-house at Ayot St Lawrence. Photo London News Agency

98　T. E. Ross reading a newspaper, while in the Tank Corps, and a postscript to one of his letters written at about the same time. Courtesy of Mrs Hilda Sims

99　T. E. Ross talking to motorcycle manufacturer George Brough. Photo courtesy of Mr and Mrs T. W. Beaumont

100　The book room at Clouds Hill, Dorset. Photo courtesy of Mrs Hilda Sims

101　T. E. Shaw at Miranshah. *National Portrait Gallery, London*

103　Aircraftman Shaw in 'scruff order', during his time in India. Photo Radio Times Hulton Picture Library

104　A snapshot of friends of T.E. standing in front of a flying boat. Photo courtesy of Mr and Mrs T. W. Beaumont

105　Aircraftman Shaw with RAF officers at trials for the Schneider Trophy race in 1929.

107　Armoured target boat at Bridlington. Photo courtesy of Mr and Mrs T. W. Beaumont

108　T. E. Shaw, early in 1935. Photo courtesy of Mrs Hilda Sims

109　Page of a popular book with a chapter about T. E. Lawrence, showing his pencilled comments and corrections in text and margin. Collection of Mrs Hilda Sims. Photo Eileen Tweedy

110　Postcard from T. E. Shaw to the Sims family. Collection of Mrs Hilda Sims. Photo Eileen Tweedy

111　Headlines about T.E.'s death from the *Western Morning News and Daily Gazette*, 20 May 1935

112　Pall bearers with T. E. Lawrence's coffin. Photo British Movietone Film Library

Winston Churchill arriving at T. E. Lawrence's funeral. Photo British Movietone Film Library

Eric Kennington carving the effigy of T. E. Lawrence. Photo courtesy of Mrs Hilda Sims

# INDEX

*Figures in italic type refer to illustrations*

Tribes, such as the Motalga, are entered under 'Arab tribes'.